UNDER THE RAINBOW

Also by David Morley

Releasing Stone (Nanholme Press, 1989)
A Belfast Kiss (Smith/Doorstop, 1990)
Exile in Voronezh: Versions after Mandelstam (Littlewood Press, 1991)
Northern Stories Two, Co-editor (Littlewood Press, 1990)

UNDER THE RAINBOW

RAINBOW

WRITERS & ARTISTS IN SCHOOLS

DAVID MORLEY
EDITED BY ANDY MORTIMER

BLOODAXE BOOKS

Copyright © Northern Arts 1991.

ISBN: 1 85224 112 8.

First published 1991 by
Bloodaxe Books Ltd,
P.O. Box 1SN,
Newcastle upon Tyne NE99 1SN,
in association with
Northern Arts,
9/10 Osborne Terrace,
Jesmond,
Newcastle upon Tyne NE2 1NZ.

Bloodaxe Books Ltd acknowledges
the financial assistance of Northern Arts.

Cover reproduction by V & H Reprographics, Newcastle upon Tyne.

Typesetting by EMS Phototypesetting, Spittal, Berwick upon Tweed.

Printed in Great Britain by
Bell & Bain Limited, Glasgow, Scotland.

Contents

When textile designer and fabric maker Mary Spyrou held a craft and design residency at Charlotte Mason College, Ambleside, she worked with children and staff in two craft workshops at Lowca Primary School and Tomlinson Junior School in Cumbria.

Acknowledgements

This publication has been achieved through the efforts of a great many people committed to the creation of closer understanding and co-operation between professional arts practitioners and schools who gave freely their valuable time, experience and knowledge. Northern Arts would like to gratefully acknowledge the support, advice and assistance of the following:

Local Education Authorities: Cleveland County, Cumbria, Durham County, Gateshead, Newcastle upon Tyne, North Tyneside, Northumberland, South Tyneside, and Sunderland.

Artists in Schools Project Steering Group: Neil Astley, Jenny Attala, Chris Bostock, Dee Dine, Malcolm Lockey (chair), Andy Mortimer, Laurie Short, and Vivienne Sillar.

The participants at the *Artists in Schools* Conference, Darlington Arts Centre, November-December 1988. Rod Taylor (Wigan LEA) who opened the Conference.

Artists' Agency, Artists in Education Training Porject, the Arts Council of Great Britain, Arts in Education for West Cumbria, Black Arts Alliance, National Foundation for Educational Research, Northern Association of Writers in Education, Northumberland Arts in Schools Project Centre, School Curriculum Development Committee, Verbal Arts Association.

Godfrey Brandt (Arts Council), Cliodhna Mulhern and Josephine Burns (North West Arts), Stephen Boyce (Southern Arts), Anne Grubb (South East Arts), Yvonne Dean, Dick Downing and Jennifer Barraclough (Yorkshire Arts), Tim Challens and Ian Ford (East Midlands Arts), John Chell (Merseyside Arts), Elizabeth Owen (West Midlands Arts), Edwina Parker-Brown (Lincolnshire and Humberside Arts).

Carol Ann Bell, Debjani Chatterjee, Chris Challis, David Craig, John Killick, Graham Mort, Tony Murray, Geoffrey Holloway.

A teacher helps her pupils during a papermaking workshop run by locally based professional printer and papermaker Rachel Gibson at Fellview Infants School in Caldbeck, Cumbria.

Foreword

Under the Rainbow is about enriching children's experience of the arts through the placement of writers, artists, craftspeople and performers in schools.

It examines the benefits of past practice in the Northern Arts region and offers constructive, practical support to those organising future ventures.

The title and structure of the book are the work of David Morley, himself a poet and writer who has worked in many schools. His lively text takes account of the evidence which came from the Northern Arts Conference, *Artists in Schools*, held in Darlington in November-December 1988. Jenny Attala, then Literature Officer for Northern Arts, explains:

> Because the various collaborative projects administered by Northern Arts had become so popular, it seemed a good time to draw artists, writers and educators together to pool ideas on the development of the work. As the financial management of schools passes into their own hands, new ways of planning and funding are also likely to be needed. Increasingly, artists and teachers want to work across the art forms – and across the curriculum. A conference was therefore planned to allow the broadest range of information and debate on work in schools in the North and throughout the art forms.
>
> On the first day, over 70 artists attended and discussed a previously circulated agenda of issues aimed at bringing out the value of the work they had done – comparing successes, difficulties and aspirations.
>
> On the second day, educationists worked their way through the same agenda – again in art form groups – and gave their perspective on work achieved and on what was needed for the future.
>
> Detailed notes were taken of all discussion and written up during the days between and after the two consultation days. This book is a distillation of that material.

But it is intended that *Under the Rainbow* should be something more than just a conference report. It is hoped that it extends beyond those few days, to illustrate ways of working and types of placement that might provide other artists and educationists with stimuli and useful information to initiate or develop their own events.

It is also hoped that this book will help break down some of the barriers that often exist between the world of the school and that of the arts. As Rod Taylor, the Art Advisor for Wigan, said when he introduced the conference:

For all the advances made, particularly over the last decade or so, there
are many teachers across the country who feel that the chances of their
school having a residency are so remote as to be barely worth
considering. Similarly, the levels of funding are still such that even when
a residency does take place, it is likely to be of such short duration that
the school deems it necessary to choose target groups of maybe as few as
twenty or thirty pupils to meet and work with the artist. It is my
conviction that *all* pupils in *all* schools should have similar access to
artists and craftspeople out of a belief that they are all entitled to an
education which should help them to know, understand and enjoy the
wider world of the arts as practised by others...

That there are clear and incontrovertible benefits to be gained from
schemes was amply illustrated in the examples outlined in
Darlington and illustrated in this book. Nor were the advantages
solely restricted to pupils. Teachers, too, found regeneration and
artists developed ideas and communication skills in contact with
their extended "audience".

It should also be borne in mind that the schemes operating in the
Northern Arts region are not running in isolation. Over the past
few years they have been linked with or run parallel to the work of
other RAAs, and benefited from some of the important research,
evaluation and development carried out by national bodies like the
Arts Council of Great Britain, the Crafts Council, the School
Curriculum Development Council and the National Foundation
for Educational Research.

*Under the rainbow: as Artist in Residence at Bransty Primary School in Cumbria,
Kate Norris worked with children and staff, giving them professional advice about the
creation of a mural.*

I believe that *Under the Rainbow*, by recording the collective experience of those writers, artists, craftspeople, performers and teachers associated with Northern Arts projects, will add to this growing body of knowledge about the important role the professional artist can play in education.

ANDY MORTIMER,
Charlotte Mason College
Ambleside, Cumbria.

Footnote: The term *artist* is used for brevity throughout this book but covers those working in crafts, dance, drama/mime, music, photography/film/video, the visual arts and writing.

Another part of the mural, which extends for 200 feet around the Bransty playground. The mural theme was Children's Play. The 4ft high wall was ideally suited to this child-sized mural.

Hexham Arts Festival brought artist Rita Smith into local schools for a series of highly popular craft workshops.

CHAPTER 1
Why Have an Artist in School?

An artist brings to the school a wealth of new experiences from which s/he selects, records, examines, rejects, reassesses, codes and decodes. To be witness, even in part to this process both stimulates enquiry and heightens perception. Because it is such a personal process, it can also foster in the audience the recognition of the worth of every individual.
– PAT VAN PELT, *former Art Education Officer*, ACGB

An artist in school is a catalysing force, bringing great advantages for individual pupils, the school as a whole and the community it serves.

Young people can be inspired and motivated by a residency – even by a brief visit. They can be encouraged to experiment, express their ideas fluently and acquire a new understanding and experience of their social and physical world.

Creativity, as a source of insight and power can enable young people, through the languages of the arts, to communicate more effectively, and to make sense of other people and of the world in which they live. Artists in schools can help young people to do this and thereby can promote self-expression and a wider view of society. *(not narrow - minded)*

The process, then, enables children to make sense of new ideas, words, configurations of light, sound, movement and substance, and to express that sense in their own way.

Self-expression

Coming from "outside", the artist can begin to break down the barriers between the world of school and that of the adult professional in a way that is often difficult for the teacher.

> An artist has a week to burn up a lot of energy in a short space, which teachers cannot allow themselves to do.
> – PAUL ROBINSON, *musician*

Each child's experience is unique and worth recording. The artist can convince children of this, and show them that the life of their community is something to be proud of, something that is worth telling other people about.

Artists can work with a variety of audiences. They encourage children to consider how the reader, watcher or listener interprets what they find. This extends children's understanding and makes them better able to make themselves understood.

To articulate their ideas fully, children need control of form and medium. Artists bring:

- another way of seeing;
- a command of exciting and innovative skills;
- the pleasure and satisfaction of sharing in making;
- a deep knowledge of the medium in which they work.

Artists can encourage children to take imaginative risks and develop new skills. This builds children's confidence in evaluating choices and resolving dilemmas in a supportive and stimulating way. *(problem solving)*

Wider views

The artist can also present a challenge in ways which can help children to recognise and question divisions in society including those of class, gender, ability and culture.

The arts cut across the sometimes arbitrary divisions of the curriculum. Their language often appeals intuitively to young people. Underlying attitudes can be changed by new perspectives.

The arts are not the preserve of a privileged few. Artists in Schools projects can open up opportunities for everyone.

Artists' residencies can promote a wider understanding of different cultures: here Madhu Jaiswal leads pupils from a Northumberland school in a dance workshop.

An artist can sometimes reach children experiencing difficulties. Achievement in the arts can bring self-esteem to those who have come to think of themselves as failures. Progress in communication can help in other areas of work, as Joan Sandison reports on her music project for children with learning difficulties:

> The children were lacking in self-confidence in everything they did. In the small group they felt secure and were not afraid to express themselves musically or verbally. Their confidence transferred to the normal classroom situation, and they began to contribute to class discussions voluntarily.

Residencies can also promote a wider understanding and appreciation of different cultures, by:

- challenging stereotypes;
- presenting a wide variety of cultural viewpoints.

This opens new horizons for all young people. When the artist is from a minority culture, the residency will present a positive image for them to remember.

> Black artists are role models for children. Children need to be reassured that black people write books, make art and music...Black culture is their culture too.
> – DEBJANI CHATTERJEE, *poet/cartoonist*

A class of 9-10 year olds at Wensleydale Middle School in Blyth producing their own books and cut-out models. David Haldane's writer/illustrator residency inspired some highly imaginative work at the Northumberland school.

Other advantages

Artists, teachers and pupils can benefit from collaboration in many
ways.

For the school:

- A well planned and publicised project will raise the school's
  profile in the local community.
- Exhibitions, publications or performances of children's work
  often strengthen the school's ties with the community. This
  can lead to greater prestige – especially when some permanent
  piece of artwork is made available to the public.
- The energy generated by the artist in the school need not be
  limited to the pupils who are actively involved in the project.
  The excitement spreads throughout the institution.
- If the wider school community – from governors to ancillary
  helpers – have been encouraged to feel part of the project, this
  sense of the school as a community can be strengthened.
- The artist's way of looking can stimulate others to a deeper
  appreciation of art.
- A visit or residency can encourage innovative ways of working
  within the school and provide a springboard for future
  projects.

For the teachers:

Artists by their presence in schools during projects, or even
working with teachers on in-service training days, can provide:

- An opportunity to keep up with recent developments in the
  arts.
- A positive view of the arts which stimulates a teacher's
  appreciative awareness.
- Exploration of cross-curricular links.
- A chance to work with a fellow professional in the arts in a
  concentrated way on a specialist project and using a different
  style of delivery.
- An opportunity to provide a role model for their pupils.

For the artists:

- An opportunity to reassess their work, learn from and be
  stimulated by children.
- The pleasure of sharing creativity with children.
- A chance to enthuse about and encourage understanding of
  their art form.

William Jefferies' tapestry residency at Caldew School, Dalston, Carlisle.

- The chance to experience the opportunity to receive a broader response to their work.
- The opportunity to excite the audiences of tomorrow.

What can the different art forms offer schools?

Artists are dedicated to pursuing their chosen art form to a point of excellence. Many different kinds of artists are represented in this book.

Crafts: Craftspeople can promote technical skills, methods and innovation for practical invention and design. Their classroom work can be exciting, enriching and demonstrate that art is alive in our community and cultures.

Dance: Dancers can demonstrate one of the primary forms of human expression. Moving, imitating and animating our feelings, ideas and perceptions is basic to emotional, intellectual, psychological and physical health.

Drama/Mime: Actor's techniques of role play can allow children to test the possibilities of new situations, practise and develop word and body language, and step into other people's shoes. Dramatic skills increase self-confidence and awareness, making learning easier in school and beyond.

Music: Musicians have powerful ways to enthuse young people through composing and performance. They might concentrate on making music and thereby complement a more theoretical school approach, or introduce the styles and functions of music from other cultures.

Photography/Film/Video: Photographers, film and video makers work with highly versatile technology which is central to modern communications. Their expertise can offer young people a creative and powerful way to record and examine life and experience.

Visual Arts: Visual artists can help children develop a visual language and demystify the art process. Drawing and painting – like writing and talking – allow us to convey attitudes and understanding. Development of these skills can arise from contact with a committed practitioner.

Writing: Writers can enable young people to express and value their own ideas and opinions, a prerequisite for effective communication. An exact command of language enhances work in all subjects and is at the heart of successful relationships, social and intellectual.

Conclusion

Visits and residencies bring tangible and immediate benefits and/or subtle, longer term gains for all who take part.

They make art for everyone a reality. Children may not become writers or artists as a result of artists in schools, but the experience can inform their future choices as potential consumers of the arts.

The essence of success is the co-operation of professionals with mutual recognition and complementary expertise. Artists respect teachers' roles and commitment and will want to work with children rather than teach them. To do this they need the teacher's wholehearted support.

A successful relationship can only be built if teachers and artists take a practical and methodical approach to planning projects. Proposals must be clear, so that all parties know what is expected of them. The next section, on planning and organisation, offers a guide to help ensure that the project will be successful.

Lisa Bird's residency in three schools in South Copeland during National Children's Bookweek involved mask-making, linking in with the Bookweek theme of magic and mystery.

CHAPTER 2

Getting It Right: Planning and Organisation

This chapter gives a straightforward, step-by-step account of how a school might set up a project. It is based on the collective experience of more than 150 artists and workers in education, with the firm intention of helping to get it right.

1. What is the goal?
2. What is the next step?
3. Funding the project.
4. Selecting the artist.
5. When and how the artist should be involved?
6. Who are the other essential members of the team?
7. What will help it work?
8. Selecting the participants.
9. Evaluation and follow up.

The checklist in the appendix will also help you to make sure you have covered all the essential points when you are organising a placement. Your RAA and/or LEA may also produce helpful guidelines.

1. What is the goal?

Before approaching an artist, you should have a clear idea of what you expect to get out of the visit. Consider and set down aims and objectives. Do you have a particular sort of session in mind? The artist will need carefully matching to these intentions.

Decide how you see the role of the artist. Do you want a "troubleshooter", an innovator to generate ideas, a technician to develop skills or someone who might bring fresh unity and life to the school or department?

2. What is the next step?

Decide on a visit or a residency. If it is to be a one-off visit, how do you intend to maximise the benefit through follow-up work? If the project is to continue for longer, how will you assist the artist in planning and pacing a longer-term residency?

In many RAA regions, the old pattern of one-off visits, where the artist appears and speaks to the sixth form or does a single workshop has given way to a whole spectrum of workshop-based activities which can occur inside or outside the school and offer exciting possibilities to a wide range of students. Graham Mort argues:

> Funding organisations will direct their subsidies towards more imagin-ative projects: a series of visits covering a wide range of activities…It is essential to plan visits carefully. The follow-up is just as important as the visit, which can be wasted unless afterwards handled in a sensitive and imaginitive way by the teachers involved.

3. Funding the project

There are a range of possible funding sources for you to consider and it is likely that the project will be funded on a partnership basis, with funds coming from a number of different directions. You should firstly consider how much the school itself is prepared to commit to the project. You could then approach the following:

The Local Education Authority. In some instances LEA advisers will have access to funds for Artists in Schools projects but with recent changes arising out of the Education Reform Act the situation may differ greatly from one LEA to another.

LEA funds may also be available through INSET or TVEI budgets and from other sources.

These pupils from Whitehaven and Wyndham secondary schools filmed, edited and composed the soundtrack for two music videos under the direction of Harmonie Band.

Northern Arts (and other RAAs) has funds specifically earmarked for Artists in Schools work and the appropriate Officer or Assistant may be able to advise you on their availability.

Charitable Trusts. There are many charitable trusts which support educational or arts activities though almost all find that requests for financial support far exceed the funds available. There may be local trusts which you know about; alternatively information can be obtained from public libraries.

Commercial and Private Sponsorship. Support for arts activities from the private sector has increased greatly in recent years and some companies are particularly interested in supporting projects involving young people. Information on sponsorship policies can usually be obtained from company offices, or possibly local branches. The Association for Business Sponsorship of the Arts runs an Incentive Scheme (BSIS) which can in certain special circumstances add to the funds secured from private sector sponsorship (their address can be found on page 79).

Local Authorities. While most Local Authority funding of Artists in Schools work is likely to be channelled through the Education Authority there are occasions when projects may be supported from other budgets. You could contact your Local Authority Arts Officer or Leisure and Recreation Department for further information.

Local Arts Development Agencies. The Northern region now has a network of LADAs with funds to aid local arts development. In some instances they may be able to assist in funding artists in schools projects (contact addresses on pages 64-67).

4. Selecting the artist.

The RAA is one important information resource centre and its officers may be able to offer advice or supply details of artists who work in schools. Similarly LEA Inspector/ Advisers may also have information about artists who have worked in the area before. This data may well be stored in a computer index and include details of the precise nature of the artists' work, their previous schools experience, and the kind of age range, class size and ability levels of the children they prefer to work with, etc.

Artists can also be selected by:

- Following up some of the ideas in chapter 5 of this book which gives a list of resources, including artists' groups.

- Receiving a personal recommendation, for example, from teachers in other schools.
- Reading publicity materials. Freelance artists often send mailshots to schools or LEAs, detailing the kind of work they offer, examples of their techniques, photographs of their workshops and performances, and copies of the children's work.
- Consulting directories. Writers can be contacted via their publishers whose addresses are listed in the *Writers' and Artists' Yearbook.* Alternatively, bodies like NAWE produce and distribute an important *Directory of Writers in Education* and the Northern Potters Association holds information about their members willing to work in schools.
- Reviewing planned local events. Touring artists – such as dance, drama, mime and music groups – often welcome the chance to include visits/workshops within their itinerary.
- Involving parents who are artists themselves.

A sculpture takes shape at Horton Grange School in Blyth, following a visit by artist Mike Clay.

Children from four schools in Allerdale took their work to an outdoor celebration at the end of a week of workshops with the Beasties (alias Bob Pegg and Julie Fullerton).

5. When and how the artist should be involved

The recommendations of the artists at the Darlington conference were that:

- Teachers and the other agencies involved should, early on, acquire a clear understanding about the way an artist proposed to work.
- Concrete details of budget, methods of payment, nature of groups to be involved, role of teacher, form of evaluation, resources available and space required, should all be hammered out at a planning meeting or meetings.
- At least one preliminary visit of the artist to the school would also be ideal.
- For any lengthy placement there should be provision in the budget to cover planning meetings.

Other issues likely to crop up at an early stage which might need to be resolved through discussion and negotiation include:

- clarification of the aims and objectives of the project;
- the use of the school and its environment;
- the use of outside visits;
- contact with other members of staff;
- additional or associated events like performances, exhibitions or publications.

When a school has outlined its intentions in a letter to the artist, it should set up the preliminary meeting/s (with alternative dates for both these and the project proper) well before it is hoped to stage the event. There are no hard and fast rules, but given the necessary amount of planning to be done, it is probably unlikely that it would be possible to successfully complete all the preliminary work in less than one term. In other words, projects should be planned one term, two terms or even a year in advance.

Prior to the first meeting with the artist, the school should have ascertained, either directly or indirectly through the advice of an RAA, a rate of pay. Initial approaches for grant aid, financial support, sponsorship etc., and discussion with the artist about a draft contract can then be started.

CONTRACTS

The precise nature of the contract will be dictated by the particular conditions of the residence but it should include consideration of:

- the artist's legal position relating to responsibility for children's safety, etc;
- insurance cover, for example for the artist's work or belongings (equipment) when in school;
- public liability insurance;
- rates of pay;
- approximate times and dates of work;
- provision of raw materials;
- indication of space;
- responsibility for administration;
- education/legal restrictions on employment;
- conditions of service in schools;
- requirements of project;
- responsibility of school;
- required documentation;
- copyright and reproduction issues.

A contract can be vital for the protection of the artist and the school, and should be ready for negotiation and agreement at the first planning meeting.

Further advice on these issues may be obtained from your RAA or LEA.

6. Who are the other essential members of the team?

In addition to the visiting artist, the teacher and the pupils, Artists in Schools schemes can also involve parents, other staff, head-teachers, governors, the local community, local businesses, the press and media.

Workshops outside the school day are often a successful way of extending the impact of the project. Consultation with arts centres and venues, arts in education workers, community groups and local authority arts/recreation officers, may provide more assistance.

Some artists may wish to use local museums, photographic archives, historical and industrial sites, or the local environment. Organising this side of the project – and keeping a weather eye open for funding opportunities – may be crucial for the development of a placement.

All these individuals and groups – especially the pupils – need informing about the purpose, function and method of the work.

There would seem little to be gained from bringing artists into school or placing them in front of a class when no one knows why they are there or anything about their work. Appropriate introductions and first impressions can be very important.

Over the Top Puppet Company at Delaval Middle School, Blyth.

7.   What will help it work?

In the examples of practice set out and described in the next chapter, each project underwent careful and thorough management while letting creative energy have its head. This balance – control and freedom – was essential. However, some other important factors need consideration:

Timetabling: Alterations to the timetable need to be made well before the placement occurs; this reduces friction with other staff. The rooms the artist will use should also be booked, and might need to be away from any centres of noise, such as dinner hall or gym.

Roles and discipline: Discuss this with the artist. Is the teacher to be a participant or an observer? Many artists prefer the teacher to participate like the pupils, unless they require adult assistance with a particular task.

The teacher may find an altered – but constructive – atmosphere in the classroom. Pupils may be contributing in ways which offend

History can be fun, and Theatre Centre's version shows its workings in today's multicultural society. They staged their production 'The House that Jack Built' in several Cumbrian schools.

The hands-on approach: William Jefferies' tapestry residency at Caldew School, Dalston, Carlisle.

traditional attitudes to discipline, but remember that this is an exciting time for everyone. It is often when matters seem most out of hand that the artist is exercising most control.

Artists are not surrogate teachers, and a member of staff should always be present unless specifically requested not to be by the artist beforehand. Ideally, the teacher should enjoy the opportunity to take part in the project they have initiated.

Hospitality: Well before the placement, the teacher should finalise all arrangements regarding transport, welcome, familiarisation with school, meals and accommodation.

Some artists will happily lodge with a teacher: this can be a great opportunity for discussing follow up work, but this should be checked beforehand.

Parental/governor support: If changes to the timetable are to be considered or if the artist might want children to work after normal school hours, or travel outside school grounds, parental and/or governor consent may well be required. All legal and charging implications should be checked out in advance.

8.   Selecting the participants.

The pupils targeted must really gain from the event, so careful selection is important, but this selection must include as many children as is practicable and from as wide an ability band as possible. Many of the models of good practice discussed at the Darlington conference gave illustration of how artists can cut through any destructive labelling of children, liberating each child to fulfil her or his potential.

Size of group: The group has to be small enough for each pupil to play an active role. Artists can get treated as a cultural commodity – it is important not to mistake the visit for an exercise in Billy Graham-style mass conversion, packing the assembly hall with the school's population. This might be O.K. for Ted Hughes or Kiri Te Kanawa, but it gives little contact between child and artist. Check with artists the maximum size of the group they want to work with. Aim for that figure. It *will* mean disappointment for those who aren't included – but it will also mean that those involved get the right attention. Many artists may want to meet the whole school in some informal way, possibly by calling round classrooms.

9. Evaluation and follow-up.

Evaluation: Teachers' reports or other documentation will prove a valuable resource for later projects. Evaluation is now seen as an interactive process between the artist, children, teacher or adviser. Sue Harries (National Foundation for Educational Research Steering Group) says that evaluation should:

- be flexible – responsive to the way aims and objectives are modified during a placement;
- be integral to the process of the project – internal assessment might be made by a group of pupils, by other staff, by the teacher and artist together;
- record the lessons which have been learned.

It might also include an exhibition, the production of an anthology, the performance of a show for parents and public.

If evaluation reflects the nature of the processes involved then it can clearly form an important element in any follow-up activity.

Follow-up work: Good management – including detailed nego-tiation between artist and teacher about the nature of follow-up and possible future projects with artists – can result in a placement becoming the impetus for a continuing creative teaching environ-ment.

If evaluation has sought a wide range of views about the project from children, teachers, parents, artists and includes a record of what they have achieved, through photographs, video and other means, such documentation can serve useful functions. It can assist in attracting funding for future projects. It can inform other teachers and artists and it can become a lasting celebration of the whole experience. The celebratory end is as important as the initial planning and actual working of the project.

Follow-up might also involve inviting further schemes that offer pupils alternative or contrasting experiences, ones that examine issues further or involve other art forms.

To increase such opportunities it may be helpful to give the school's staff development officer, or any other member of staff involved in administrating in-service funding, a detailed report of the outcome of the event, as well as to any of the RAA and LEA officers, artists, sponsors, governors or headteacher involved in the project.

This pebble mosaic for Flimby Primary School's nature garden was produced during Maggie Howarth's residency, one of a series of arts-based environmental projects in West Cumbria.

Pupils from Solway School in Silloth assembled a large-scale ceramic wall mural depicting their town during a residency with ceramic artist Paul Scott.

CHAPTER 3
Good Practice

Artists and teachers have their own success stories to tell. There is an enormous range of methods and styles of placement within each art form. This section shows how they might be operated in practical terms, with a single, detailed account of good practice from each art form. These examples show some ways of running successful projects. Each project is unique, but each includes all of the following elements:

- **Initiation.**
- **Planning.**
- **In Progress.**
- **Consolidation and Development.**

CRAFTS
Ceramics in Whitehaven Comprehensive School.

In August 1985, Paul Scott – a ceramicist working and living in Cumbria – responded to a listing in *Artists Newsletter*. After discussions with the Arts in Education Worker for West Cumbria, a project took shape – a residency based on Whitehaven buildings at Whitehaven Comprehensive School.

Children were to experience working with a professional artist for some length of time: one day a week for 10 weeks. Aims and objectives were carefully chosen. Children were to experience:

- The use of a camera in selecting and photographing parts of buildings of their choice in Whitehaven Town Centre.
- Making drawings on paper, relating to the buildings, doors and windows.
- Using clay, tools, glaze and underglaze to work on panels, pots, bowls and three-dimensional forms based on their drawings and photographs.
- Research into the historical details of particular buildings and their change of uses over the years.
- Being involved with the press – radio, TV, newspapers – and in the exhibiting of their work at the end of the project.

The Arts in Education Worker co-ordinated the project, and solicited funding from both public sources – Northern Arts and the LEA – and a private source, a local firm, Eskett Quarries.

> They gave seven hundred pounds, but when I told them about the Business Sponsorship Incentive Scheme (BSIS) – how the Government would match any sum they gave so long as it exceeded a thousand pounds – they increased their support by another three hundred pounds
> – VIVIENNE SILLAR

Back at the school, the planning was underway between Paul, the heads of Art and History, and Vivienne Sillar. The historical link was found hard to carry through because of staffing and timetabling difficulties. Despite this, the project took shape:

> It involved one group of third year pupils. Eighty wanted to join – sixteen were selected…for their willingness to stick with a long project
> – PAUL SCOTT

In July, Paul answered questions from parents – they were concerned about missed lessons. He outlined the project, talked about his own work and the scope of the residency, and his description reassured them of its value. Because parents were involved at an early stage, they could make suggestions about places in the town to visit and photograph. Parents also gave consent for their children to be allowed outside school during normal hours.

During the first three project days, pupils spent the afternoons photographing and drawing in Whitehaven. The first morning was

spent arranging the studio space, after which the sequence of the residency involved:

> Photographing (in town centre) ● Drawing on paper (scale drawings, pencil, crayon, paint) ● Making terraced plant pot holders (experimenting with drawing in clay, impressed decoration, using the glaze and underglaze colours) ● Making relief panels of chosen doors, windows or buildings (referring to photographs and drawings) ● Painting and glazing panels ● Moulded/constructed plates, trays and dishes ● Painting and glazing (using images from photographs and drawings).

The children also paid visits to local architects and a museum. They were interviewed by Radio Cumbria, BBC Television, *The Guardian* and Whitehaven newspapers. The residency was videoed by other pupils as part of a GCSE assignment.

After the work from the residency was exhibited at Whitehaven School, it was then taken to Whitehaven Civic Hall for its first public showing. This was a larger exhibition – it included documentation in the form of photographs and statements from pupils, teachers and the artist himself.

> The whole project injected interest, discussion and enthusiasm about art which acted as a stimulus in the normal day to day work of the department.
>
> – ELAINE LANE, *Art teacher*

Eskett Quarries, the principal sponsor, were presented with an award for their initiative by Richard Luce, the Arts Minister. Additionally, the company funded the event's buffet on the

condition that it was prepared by the school's Home Economics students – this gave them a rare opportunity to cater for over 150 people and reinforced the commitment the company gave to the school.

Paul Scott was also commissioned to produce a ceramic panel for the school. This was the task he chose to do during his own studio sessions in the school and the pupils were able to witness its development alongside their own work.

Such was the success of the residency – and the quality of the children's work – that an exhibition and summary project was presented at a National Association for Education in the Arts conference in London.

DRAMA

Prism Theatre Group working with children with special needs.

The project started with a visit by Prism Theatre to a special needs school in the small rural market town of Wigton. This had been initiated by the Arts in Education worker for West Cumbria in response to the headteacher's wish to enrich her pupils' curriculum through a programme of arts experience.

The headteacher invited Prism, who specialise in working with disabled and handicapped people, to set up a project. Support was also invited from third year Arts students on a B.Ed. course at Charlotte Mason College, as part of their school-based experience. Other participants were children from another special school, a small group of older pupils from a tutorial centre who had behavioural difficulties, and a complete top junior class from the neighbouring mainstream primary school.

So the event involved a rich mixture of ages (4 to 17), and abilities (from the most able to those with moderate or severe learning difficulties). As well as introducing the work of pro-fessional actors and musicians to the children, the project allowed the staff and students involved to examine some of the practical issues implicit within an LEA policy of special needs integration.

At a planning meeting of all the staff/providers involved, it was agreed to cover the costs by forming a partnership funding structure. Each participating school contributed a small sum from their INSET budget or other source. This was then matched by money from the College of Higher Education and, in turn, the Arts

in Education Worker matched this total amount with industrial and trust sponsorship topped up with an RAA grant. Some materials were supplied by local industry, and the scene was set for the project to begin.

Eight consecutive Tuesdays were identified on which the students would have responsibility for the morning sessions and Prism would run the afternoons. The two parts of the day were linked thematically and by the fact that all the activities were to come together at the end of the project in a performance and participatory event. Prism's role was very much to be the catalyst for the theme and for the form of this finale.

At a preliminary meeting Prism introduced the student teachers and teachers to their work and the framework for the project and detailed ideas for follow-up work were discussed. One student took on the role of evaluator and recorder, and a photographic and video record of the project was kept as well as interviews conducted with pupils, teachers and assistants. The setting for the project was the hall and two large classrooms in the special school which was the most central site for all the participants.

The first appearance of the theatre group – bedecked in multi-coloured coats and acting as part of a lost troupe of travelling entertainers who had been shipwrecked nearby – mesmerised the children. They taught them songs, led dances and movement sequences and invited the pupils to help them devise a festivity to celebrate the arrival of Spring. This theme was taken up by the

The arrival of Spring: a dance workshop with Prism.

students as the guide to the activities they organised on each subsequent morning session.

Most of this work was based on visual art – making large spring flowers that would open up; producing an elaborate collage mural with spring birds and beasts in a local landscape; turning the school hall into a 3-D environment with clouds, sunshine, rainshowers and rainbow; and masks for the dancers.

Gradually the supporting art work, and the environment, came to completion. Prism worked with the groups of children, sometimes together, sometimes in smaller groups, to perfect the music, the dance, the mime and the drama that would depict the triumph of Spring over Winter. The repertoire of celebratory songs was extended. Children explored appropriate gestures and movements until, after eight days of hard work and fun, the theatre group led the final afternoon's wonderful performance. The atmosphere was magical.

Whilst all this activity went on, some less obvious, but nevertheless remarkable, changes were taking place. Not only were physical skills and knowledge being developed, but social skills, attitudes and values were undergoing major shifts. As one pupil from the mainstream school explained:

> I was a bit worried at first about working with disabled children, but after the first two days I soon started to get used to it…and I didn't really notice that they were handicapped or anything…it just seemed that there wasn't any difference between us really.

Other pupils from the primary school reported that they met the special school children in the local swimming baths and went to talk to them – something they wouldn't have done before the Prism project.

One of the boys from the tutorial centre told his teacher that he now realised that he wasn't so badly off as he originally thought and he now appreciated how good it was to be able 'to think for yourself'.

Members of staff from the special schools noticed that one of their pupils, from being a "non-speaking" child, with Prism's help began to offer conversation voluntarily and stopped having to stay near one of her teachers. Another child 'actually sat down at a table and worked with other children for the first time'.

These observations would appear to be eloquent proof of the success of the project. They also reinforce the potential of drama and theatre as a powerful arts medium to bring about a change in attitude.

MUSIC

Composing for a Silent Film in West Cumbria

Paul Robinson was appointed Northern Arts Composer Fellow at Newcastle University in 1985. He contacted Arts in Education Worker, Vivienne Sillar, in October of that year with a proposal to run a week of "composing for film" workshops. He wanted the Harmonie Band – a group of six musicians – to come to West Cumbria and work with children towards a final performance of their own composition. The aim was to use the children as the focus of the week's residency.

Vivienne Sillar acted as the broker between the artists, schools and funding bodies. Many organisations contributed financially – Northern Arts, Cumbria LEA, Copeland Borough Council, Allerdale District Council, Michael Tippett Musical Foundation, Hinrichsen Trust, Ralph Vaughan Williams Trust, Musician's Union and The Performing Rights Society – the latter's contribution was made possible by all its composer, author and publisher members voluntarily giving up a part of their annual royalties.

The agreed aim of the project was to demonstrate the important part music has to play when heard on film. The schedule involved four demonstration/performances in different primary schools in the mornings. The afternoons were spent in the same secondary school where each musician was timetabled to work with one group of ten pupils.

Instruments were supplied by both the band and the schools. The film – a 1923 silent movie – was brought along by the

musicians, assisted by a technician.

Preparation included an initial meeting with all the teachers involved in the project to tell them what they would be seeing and hearing in the performance. Paul Robinson met these teachers and showed a video of the ensemble performing with *Paris Qui Dort.* He then gave all the teachers exercises which could be carried out with the pupils before the visit. This helped the children to be aware of the role of music when heard with film.

The six musicians and technician worked and lived in West Cumbria for the week. In the mornings they toured the four primary schools performing their own score, specially written for the film, while the film was screened; in the afternoons they did a workshop with 60 pupils at Wyndham School, Egremont – the children collectively devised their own version of the score. On the final afternoon, these pupils performed their own composition for a film to an audience of 200 first year children:

> I was amazed when I saw how you played them. The film was good with the music you played. Afterwards, I tried to think what it would have been like without it…I was astounded.

The success of the project not only lay with the talent of the ensemble for communicating with young people, but also with the immensely detailed planning and organisation, much of which was done by Paul Robinson and Vivienne Sillar.

After the project was finished, the children wrote essays about it, giving their impressions, and Paul Robinson visited the secondary school to discuss the project with staff and pupils. He gave them a copy of the entire film so that they could carry on working with it in more detail.

PHOTOGRAPHY

Are We Being Watched? A Photographer's Residency.

Mik Critchlow, an experienced photographer based in North-umberland, was invited into Coquet High School in Amble to work with staff and pupils:

- to help pupils make a photographic record of the townscape and people of Amble;
- to provide expertise, ideas, information and support for photography within the TVEI programme, staff INSET and community workshops;
- to help staff develop materials and resources in collaboration with an experienced photographer;
- to assist in the integration of photography within the 14+ curriculum.

How did he do this? Whilst in school, Mik worked with staff and pupils recording everyday life in the modern, thriving comprehensive school. He then took students out of doors into the town and

helped them to discriminate between subjects for photography, using qualities of light, composition and balance.

The school wanted to set up a darkroom – who better than Mik to assist staff in choosing and buying the appropriate materials and equipment? The darkroom became a long-term resource – useful for showing pupils novel ways of developing their own prints. These prints were then used to mount an exhibition in the school.

> We now have a fully operational darkroom available and the staff confidence and enthusiasm to build on the success of the residency. The standard of work produced by the students and their new skills and confidence with the medium of photography proves how valuable the residency has been.
>
> – STEVE QUINLAN, *Deputy Head*

As well as supporting work within the TVEI programme, GCSE assignments, staff in-service and community workshops, Mik was invited back to act as Picture Editor on the school's first community newspaper venture when the people of Amble were able to see for themselves the skill of the young photographers.

DANCE

Creative Dance Project in Northumberland: South Beach First School, Blyth

As part of the SCDC Arts in Schools Initiative in Northumberland a professional dancer, Barbara Slater from the Clann Na Gael Irish Dance Group worked with children and dance teacher and artist Jan Rule to develop a strategy for dance for the whole school.

The first part of the project involved a group of fifth year pupils who had experienced dance as part of their PE curriculum. The work took place during the summer term of 1987 building on the children's country dance knowledge and exploring folk traditions and customs.

Children studied the traditions of costume, food, music and stories in their own area and culture. To prepare for the creative dance element a series of events were held including a maypole dancing club, May Day festivities and the making and designing of costumes. At this point the professional dancer, Barbara Slater, joined the project introducing children to soft shoe steps, Ceilidh, hard shoe dancing and Gaelic costume design. This enjoyable experience not only created enormous enthusiasm for using the dance steps which they learnt (and taught to other children at playtimes), but also extended further the cultural horizons of the project.

At this stage the dance work was linked to visual art, with the exploration and creation of shapes and forms in a gallery of living sculptures.

The two elements, creative dance and visual arts, were combined in a series of exercises based on close observation from chosen viewpoints using sketches and cut-out techniques. After some experimentation, photography was also used as a means of selecting and storing images.

To introduce direct recording in visual terms the children were asked to respond to a variety of simple musical instruments through movement. Word association was introduced to give an extra dimension to the children's response.

The elements of this cross art form work were brought together in a large class book and a frieze showing the kinds of movements generated by a single instrument. Another frieze – recorded in silhouettes – formed a variety of dance shapes produced by the children. Country dance, creative dance and visual arts projects continued to develop within formal lessons and extra curricular activities within the school.

Dance projects such as this work extremely well when tied in with one or more subjects so as to become part of the curriculum – residencies can provide a big and bold starter project for a long-term programme of continued dancing.

VISUAL ARTISTS

Swimming with paint: Visual Arts and Special Needs

David Swift was the holder of the Northern Arts Craft Residency funded by Cumbria County Council and Northern Arts, and based at Cumbria College of Art in 1987. Shortly after his appointment, he was invited to Whitehaven to visit Mayfield School with a view to undertaking a five-day residency there. David had expressed a particular interest in working with children with special needs, although he had no experience at that time of this type of work.

On touring round the school, the headteacher showed David the Hydrotherapy Pool which was used by the children daily. The pool was kept at a high temperature to allow easy movement but was housed in a bare and clinical room.

It was decided that David would work with the children to create a narrative scene around the walls of the pool. Originally the theme of 'Jungle' was chosen. This was later changed to 'The Sea' as it allowed better scope for the pupils to add texture – being a looser way to work and not being too limited by the space of the background wall. David adapted a few of his original ideas when he realised how the situation would dictate certain constraints.

Since David was based at the art college, he had regular contact with students. It transpired that one of them – Ashley Latimer – had a great deal of experience with special needs children. She was co-opted on to the residency to assist David.

Ashley turned out to be a great asset to the project – she and

David worked out the basic design of the mural over the weekend prior to the children coming back to school. However, extra motifs could be added at the request of the children, and so the mural grew from their interest. While David was responding to requests for sharks and mermaids, Ashley worked directly with the children, helping them to make textures of water and seaweed using their fingers and sponges. Two areas of work – David's and the children's – merged well and worked as one image.

There were no obvious distinctions between the professional art work and the children's. About eight children took part in contributing to the mural – a small number, but each child had one-to-one attention while Ashley helped them. Many of the children had severe communication problems, unable to speak or to see. However, the pleasure and intense involvement was clearly visible in each child. Most obvious was the excitement generated in the staff and pupils who were using the pool. The room itself now feels much larger, and seems to have a distance about it where before it felt closed in.

The visual stimulus of the mural is used by the staff – who before could really only talk about movement with the children. Now there are several points of discussion motivated by the images on the walls. The children themselves have obvious delight in looking at their favourite sections:

> One boy simply wanted to look constantly, and a shark was specially painted at his request. He talked about it always as he played in the water.
>
> – VIVIENNE SILLAR

Martyn Wiley leads a Circus of Poets writing workshop at St Patrick's RC Junior School, Cleator Moor.

WRITING

Writing and Science in Jarrow.

St Bede's RC Junior School, Jarrow, used the Writers in Schools scheme for the first time in 1989. The address of the writer was given by the Literature Officer of Northern Arts. The poet's brief wasn't strict – he was given a free hand to develop a cross-curricular set of techniques he'd found useful for juniors.

The costs for this residency incorporated the writer's fee for two days in school, travelling expenses and an INSET workshop for local teachers. This was negotiated between the LEA adviser, the writer and Northern Arts. South Tyneside LEA and Northern Arts funded the project on a 50/50 basis.

Pupils were expecting two days of poetry – the teacher had already primed them with the writer's work. Instead, they were blindfolded while the teacher and the poet placed badgers, foxes, magpies, hares and rabbits on their desks (all items on free loan from Tyne & Wear Museum Service).

After this initial surprise, the children began to look at the animals in a new way – most of them had never been this close to a creature before. The poet introduced the theme of co-operation – how each animal species is interdependent – by getting the children to talk about their own inner-city environment.

He then used "gospel" – question and response – to encourage the children to think about how their animal perceived its world. The children were given a series of questions – Who am I? What am I like? How are things from my point of view? – and made notes about the animal before them.

They were then shown slides of the environment their animals lived in. The poet play-acted each animal in turn so the children got an idea of its behaviour. The children were then encouraged to adopt their animal as a role model – to "get inside its skin" using whatever means they had available, apart from literally! The introduction of metaphor and simile – and brainstorming for imagery – was crucial to make this imaginative leap.

By this time the class had a wealth of notes about the natural world which would have pleased any A-Level Biology teacher. After playing word games, and listening to the poet's work, the children began writing their own poems using the question and answer form to explore different perspectives:

The Hare – Daniel Harbinson (10)

What am I like?

I am like a ball of hay
with pointed ears like big bullets.
I have eyes as if they had polish on,
and teeth like little sharp knives.

The Hare – David Hutchinson (11)

What am I like?

I am like a ball of wool,
but really,
I have eyes as coloured as cars,
but small like stars.
My teeth as white as a sheet,
I'm dying to eat a lot
I'm starving as you can see.
My scut flashes and flicks
like a small lighthouse.
My ears as pointy as a knife.
My ears as long as a pencil and as wide as two fingers,
but like a leaf.

This process of looking, touching, researching and writing continued over another day – with the writer holding one-to-one workshops with each child. The workshops were used to share new ideas about the behaviour of living creatures in the modern world – with stress on environmental issues such as the ozone layer.

Lisa Bird worked with David Swift in a residency at St James C. of E. School in Whitehaven, building upon the children's previous classroom work on insects and millicreatures. This photograph shows one of the three-dimensional fantasy creatures made during the two artists' week in the school.

Textile residency in a Northumberland school.

CHAPTER 4

Summary: Functions & Styles

What is apparent from the examples in Chapter 3, and from other projects described at the Northern Arts Darlington Conference, is that placements of this sort have a variety of functions.

Artists in Schools projects can:

- Share with children the risks and rewards involved in making the arts.
- Enthuse young people with the joy of creating.
- Encourage pupils to develop a greater understanding of the processes involved in making objects, communicating ideas and expressing feelings.
- Demonstrate how source material is used to inspire new work by introducing pupils to the new environments from which artists draw their ideas.
- Enrich children's experience of their own environment, revealed afresh through the work of the visitor.
- Remove the blinkers of our own cultures and open up new worlds.
- Show how links may be formed across art forms and across other traditional "subject" boundaries.
- Introduce pupils to new skills or develop existing ones.
- Allow a child's mind to be engaged on a concentrated task over a longer period of time than usual – conventional ideas about a child's "attention span" are often challenged by work of this kind.
- Develop pupils' self-esteem by having their work played, performed or exhibited alongside that of professionals.
- Bring together people of different ages, of different abilities or from different schools to work on a joint task, share common experiences and develop mutual understanding.
- Refresh the commitment or update the artistic skills of teachers.
- Establish or reinforce links between a school and its local industry, arts centre, museum, library etc, through joint involvement in a project.

- Provide, through the example or input of the specific artist, links with other events (concerts, performances, exhibitions, festivals).
- Leave behind, long after the visit or residency has finished, a tangible outcome of the artist's endeavour – perhaps in the form of a commissioned piece of work for the school or community.
- Raise the profile of a particular art form in a school, group of schools or community.
- Whet appetites for a permanent engagement with the work of that artist or others working in similar or different ways.
- Increase awareness of what it means to be a "professional artist".

Sometimes some of these things happen in schools as a result of good teaching BUT many *more* of them happen *frequently* when artists are brought into schools.

At the Darlington Conference artists and educationalists also identified four distinctive "styles" of placement. The effectiveness of these might be considered in relation to the function of the project.

The commonest ways of working in schools were:

- A "looking-over-the-shoulder" style where pupils received little or no direct instruction from the artist. The child was simply a witness to an artist's thinking process, creative act or work pattern.
- A "half-and-half" approach, in which part of the artist's time was spent on their own work (witnessed and often paralleled by the pupils) whilst the remaining time was involved in directing children's work.
- A 100% involvement by the artist in directing children's work on a project agreed between them and the teacher.
- A gradual and developing involvement which extended from a growing assimilation of pupil needs by the artist and an increased understanding of the artist's technique by the pupils.

Short visits, a series of workshops or a longer full-time residency could all be carried out in one of these "styles".

In addition, the child's developing understanding might come about as a result of a "block" experience or as part of a "drip-feed" programme.

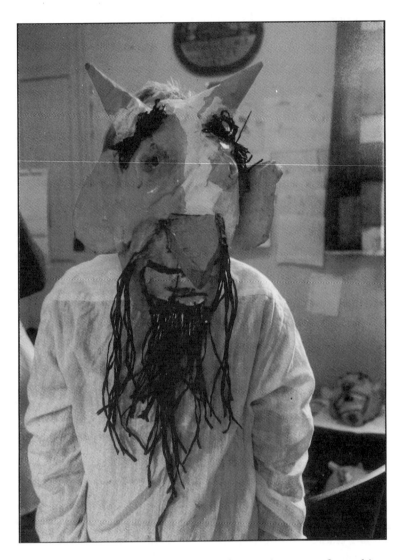

Such a rich variety of reasons for and ways of working demands the closest of co-operation and thorough planning before and throughout a project. It is hoped that the examples and guidelines given in this book will help that process and encourage artists and teachers alike to help children benefit from meeting and working with ARTISTS IN SCHOOLS.

CHAPTER 5

Who Can Help?: Resources

A list of organisations in the Northern region which might be of assistance to you in planning a project is given below. The list includes:

A   1. Northern Arts.
    2. Performing companies and artists' groups – by art form.
    3. Other agencies.
    4. LADAs.

There are other sources of advice and information outside the region:

B   1. National arts bodies.
    2. National research and funding agencies.
    3. Regional Arts Associations.
    4. Other national and regional arts agencies.
    5. Publications and reports.

A

1. Northern Arts

This is the second largest of England's twelve Regional Arts Associations and serves the counties of Durham, Cumbria, Northumberland, Cleveland and the five metropolitan districts of Tyne and Wear. Northern Arts is a company limited by guarantee which is funded by the Arts Council of Great Britain, the British Film Institute, the Crafts Council and the local authorities of the Northern region.

Northern Arts operates as a funding and development agency for the North of England, supporting a range of major arts-producing, promoting and exhibiting organisations across the visual and performing arts, regional arts development agencies such as Equal Arts (formerly Northern Shape) and Folkworks and many individual artists through a range of support schemes. In partnership with local authorities Northern Arts funds and works closely with a range of Local Arts Development Agencies in developing the arts at local level, and with Education Authorities in supporting arts in education initiatives.

Northern Arts has a team of specialist officers who are able to give advice and assistance across a range of art forms. A slide index of work by visual artists, craftspeople and photographers is maintained at Northern Arts and is open to view.

Other Regional Arts Associations are listed on pages 73-74.

Northern Arts
9/10 Osborne Terrace,
Jesmond,
Newcastle upon Tyne NE2 1NZ.
☎ 091-281 6334.
FAX 091-281 3276.

2. Performing Companies and Artists' Groups in the Northern Region

CRAFTS

Cumbria Craft Guild
Mr Gordon Pitt,
Dawson Fold,
Lyth Valley,
Kendal,
Cumbria.
Secretary to the regional multi-craft guild.

Northern Potters Association
Janina Emery,
Secretary,
Hill Top Farm,
Hurworth,
Darlington,
Co Durham DL2 2EG
☎ 0325-721064.
A non-selective association of potters and those interested in ceramics whose aim is to promote pottery through exhibitions, demonstrations and educational residencies in the Northern region. Has experience in school residencies.

DANCE & MIME

Virginia Taylor
7 Church Flags,
Kirkby Stephen,
Cumbria CA17 4RA.
☎ 07683-72053.
Virginia Taylor is a professional dancer and choreographer, who runs Cumbria Dance Project. CDP has a particular interest in promoting creative residencies in schools and colleges and Virginia is keen to undertake projects in all of the five Northern Arts regions.

Cleveland
Cleveland Dance Project
Mosaic Dance Centre,
2a Exchange Square,
Middlesbrough,
Cleveland TS1 1DN.
☎ 0642-241553.

Cumbria
Cumbria Dance Project
Virginia Taylor,
7 Church Flags,
Kirkby Stephen,
Cumbria CA17 4RA.
☎ 07683-72053.
CDP is led by professional dancer and choreographer Virginia Taylor, who has over the past 15 years initiated and responded to an enormous range of educational creative and "outreach' projects, nationally and internationally. Working with primary schools through to students on MA dance courses from single sessions to term (long cross) curriculum projects.
    CDP has some funding to undertake work within Cumbria, but VT is happy to undertake other projects elsewhere.

Mime
Debi Barnard/Alicyn Marr,
Broadthorn Cottage,
Mealbank,
Skelsmergh,
Kendal,
Cumbria.

Durham
Tandem Dance
Trish Winter,
Fowlers Yard,
Back Silver Street,
Durham.
☎ 091-386 8176.

Northumberland
Northumberland Dance Project
Andrew Ormston,
Northumberland Arts Officer,
County Central Library,
The Willows,
Morpeth,
Northumberland NE61 1TA.
☎ 0670-512385.
FAX 0670-518012.

Employs a full-time dance artist in residence. Co-ordinates dance in schools and the community including youth dance, residencies and work with promoters.

Northumberland Schools Dance Association (NSDA)
Andrew Ormston,
Northumberland Arts Officer,
County Central Library,
The Willows,
Morpeth,
Northumberland NE61 1TA.
☎ 0670-512385.
FAX 0670-518012.

Aims to stimulate and provide dance activity in a schools and curriculum context through working closely with teachers in Northumberland. NSDA was involved with the region's first dance festival, the National Youth Dance Festival, in Hexham.

Tyne & Wear

Dance City
Sarah Dabell,
Dance Development Worker,
Peel Lane,
Off Waterloo Street,
Newcastle upon Tyne NE1 4DW.
☎ 091-261 0505.

Dance City offer a range of dance activities for the general public as well as specific classes for schools, colleges, youth, community and special needs groups. Residency work with professional artists includes visits to schools.

Splinter Group Mime
Ouseburn Warehouse,
Level 4,
36 Lime Street,
Byker,
Newcastle upon Tyne NE1 2PQ.
☎ 091-261 9230.

DRAMA

Tyne & Wear
Backworth Drama Centre
Spike Hale,
Church Road,
Backworth,
Whitley Bay,
Tyne & Wear NE27 0JE.

Tyne & Wear Theatre in Education
Chris Bostock,
Director,
67a Westgate Road,
Newcastle upon Tyne NE1 1SG.
☎ 091-232 3366.
FAX 091-261 9699.

The group tours Theatre in Education programmes to infant, junior and secondary schools and presents plays for young people between ages 2 and 18. The company attends regular open meetings of Teachers Forum and resource materials are shared with schools.

Live Theatre Co.
Dave Clarke,
Administrator,
8 Trinity Chare,
Quayside,
Newcastle upon Tyne NE1 3DF.
☎ 091-261 2694.

Productions are commissioned from Northern playwrights and feature mainly actors and other theatre professionals native to the region. Most productions are for general adult audiences. They have their own small theatre on the Quayside.

Durham
Durham Theatre Co.
Artistic Director,
Darlington Arts Centre,
Vane Terrace,
Darlington,
Co Durham DL3 7AX.
☎ 0325-469861.

Small scale, community company touring two professional productions each year. Mounts a community production for presentation in Durham Cathedral and operates a youth residency at the Darlington Arts Centre.

Durham County Drama Centre
Warden,
Arthur Pease Building,
Trinity Road,
Darlington,
Co. Durham DL3 7AZ.
☎ 0325-465935.

The Centre offers in-service training for teachers, exam classes in drama/theatre, leisure classes in drama for 5 years to adult and is a resource centre.

Cumbria

Pocket Theatre Co.
Artistic Director,
Morley Street,
Carlisle,
Cumbria CA2 5HQ.
☎ 0228-512787.

Cumbria's professional touring theatre group presenting work across a broad dramatic range. Undertakes drama workshops with schools.

Northumberland

Northumberland Theatre Co.
Administrator,
The Playhouse,
Bondgate Without,
Alnwick,
Northumberland NE66 1PQ.
☎ 0665-602586.

The professional theatre service of Northumberland and the Scottish Borders, servicing schools and community venues.

Cleveland
Cleveland Theatre Co.
Alasdair Ramsay,
Artistic Director,
c/o Dovecot Arts Centre,
Dovecot Street,
Stockton-on-Tees,
Cleveland TS18 1LL.
☎ 0642-611625.

Community Theatre Companies
Bruvvers
Michael Mould,
Director,
Top Floor,
Ouseburn Warehouse Workshops,
36 Lime Street,
Byker,
Newcastle upon Tyne NE1 2PQ.
☎ 091-261 9230.

Newcastle's own Theatre and Community Arts Company. Cultural provision for the disadvantaged in the inner city. National and international contacts over two decades of work in the North East.

Middle/Large Scale
Production Companies

Northern Stage
Artistic Director,
67a Westgate Road,
Newcastle upon Tyne NE1 1SG.
☎ 091-232 3366.

The region's largest production theatre company. The company has no base theatre and therefore uses a range of different venues to present innovative and challenging new work.

Century Theatre
(Blue Box Company)
The Lakeside,
Keswick,
Cumbria LA12 5DJ.
☎ 0596-72282.

Specialist and Other Companies

Dodgy Clutch Theatre Company
Elaine Beard,
11c Akenside Terrace,
Jesmond,
Newcastle upon Tyne NE2 1TN.
☎ 091-281 4016.
Much work with schools.

Living Memory Theatre
7 Stratford Grove West,
Newcastle upon Tyne NE6 5BB.
☎ 091-261 1031.

N.E. Puppet Company
c/o Mid Northumberland Arts Group,
Town Hall,
Ashington,
Northumberland NE63 8RX.

Over the Top Puppet Company
Eileen Hares,
Co-Director,
1 Tindale Terrace,
Tindale Fell,
Brampton,
Cumbria CA8 2QJ.
☎ 06976-373.
Puppet-making and performance workshops for all ages. Have participated in Arts in Schools projects and other residencies in Northern schools, stimulating cross-curricular activities. Puppet shows for 3-12 year olds. Experience with teachers' INSET days.

Prism Theatre
Pack Horse Lane,
English Street,
Carlisle,
Cumbria CA3 8JP.
☎ 0228 819989.
Prism Theatre run practical, creative sessions for young people with different educational needs. Using different creative arts, the sessions complement the requirements of the national curriculum and foster co-operation and the development of new skills.

LITERATURE

Northern Playwrights Society
John Eden,
3 Moore Court,
Newburn,
Newcastle upon Tyne NE15 8QE.
☎ 091-267 6181.

Membership of working playwrights, theatre professionals & amateurs and other interested individuals and organisations. Object to promote and protect playwrights in the Northern Arts region.

The Mighty Pen
Northumberland Arts Officer,
County Central Library,
The Willows,
Morpeth,
Northumberland NE61 1TA.
☎ 0670-512385.
FAX 0670-518012.

Provides a year round programme of literature and poetry related work in schools and libraries, targeted at specific groups. The work links with Community Health Centres, community groups, schools and youth projects throughout Northumberland.

MUSIC

Northern Sinfonia
Jane Charlton,
Education Officer,
41 Jesmond Vale,
Newcastle upon Tyne NE2 1PG.
☎ 091-232 2108.

In addition to its concert programme the Northern Sinfonia undertakes some educational work and has details of professional musicians based in the North.

PHOTOGRAPHY, FILM & VIDEO

Darlington Media Group
Paul Dillon,
Darlington Arts Centre,
Vane Terrace,
Darlington,
Co. Durham DL3 7AX.
☎ 0325-488139.

Democratic voluntary organisation which runs an open access community darkroom and print shop. Cheap facilities and materials offered to groups and individuals. Free advice given on media matters, in particular photography. Have worked with playschemes and other children's groups and can adapt workshops to suit special needs groups.

Dovecot Cinema and Darkroom
Paul Mellor,
Film and Photography Officer,
Dovecot Arts Centre,
Dovecot Street,
Stockton-on-Tees,
Cleveland TS18 1LL.
☎ 0642-611625.

Northumberland Video Project
Northumberland Arts Officer,
County Central Library,
The Willows,
Morpeth,
Northumberland NE61 1TA.
☎ 0670-512385.
FAX 0670-518012.

Provides video facilities (including an S-VHS Edit Suite) for schools and community groups in Northumberland. This is an extension of the County Library's Community Resources Programme.

Jack Drum Entertainment
Julie Ward or Paddy Burton,
8 Charles Terrace,
Pelton Fell,
Chester-le-Street,
Co. Durham DH2 2RE.
☎ 091-389 3128.

Company specialising in participatory arts activity. Projects can include music, drama, creative writing, puppet, banner and model-making. Multimedia work a speciality. Experience of Multimedia workshops with school children and teachers.

Projects UK
1 Black Swan Court,
Westgate Road,
Newcastle upon Tyne NE1 1SG.
☎ 091-232 2410.

Projects UK promotes new and innovative work in the contemporary arts and media specialising in photography, performance (visual arts based), sound and vision. The organisation undertakes training work at its Newcastle base and maintains information and resources in the above areas of activity.

Welfare State International
P.O. Box 9,
Ulverston,
Cumbria LA12 1AA.
☎ 0229-57146.

Celebratory Arts Company working on a variety of projects with schools. Offering in-service training days for teachers.

3. Other Agencies in the Region

AN Publications
Production Editor,
P.O. Box 23,
Sunderland,
Tyne & Wear SR4 6DG.
☎ 091-567 3589.
FAX 091-510 9637.

AN Publications provides an information service for artists and visual arts organisations. It publishes handbooks, directories and a monthly magazine *Artists Newsletter*, which lists residencies for artists, craftspeople and photographers and often contains reports on residencies and artists-in-schools projects. Back issues of the newsletter are available containing articles and reports on *all* aspects of residencies including children with special needs and multicultural projects.

Artists' Agency
1/2 Floor,
16 Norfolk Street,
Sunderland SR1 1EA.
☎ 091-510 9318.

Artists' Agency promotes participation in the arts through the creation of closer links between practising artists and the public primarily through placements but also involvement with other projects. The Agency's work is not focussed on educational establishments alone but it does maintain details of artists experienced in residency work and is a source of expertise in this field.

Arts in Education
West Cumbria
Carol Ann Bell,
Arts in Education Worker,
Rosehill Theatre,
Moresby,
Whitehaven,
Cumbria CA28 6SE.
☎ 0946 694558.

Arts in Education is responsible for initiating arts-based projects within education where professional artists have the opportunity to work with young people and teachers.

Brewery Photography
Gallery & Workshop
Stan Taylor and Michael Watts,
122a High-water,
Kendal,
Cumbria LA9 4HE.
☎ 0539-725133.

The Brewery Arts Centre in Kendal presents a combination of professional performances and amateur participatory activity including theatre, music, film, exhibitions and workshops.

Equal Arts
(formerly Northern Shape)
Whinney House,
Durham Road,
Gateshead,
Tyne & Wear NE9 5AR.
☎ 091-487 8892 – voice and minicoms.

Equal Arts is the Northern region's arts and disability agency working towards greater equality of opportunity within the arts for disabled people and people with special needs in partnership with statutory and voluntary agencies. Equal Arts can provide information and examples of placement and residencies in special schools or with pupils with disabilities and special needs. They can also offer special advice on setting up a specific project, e.g. funding, suitable artists, structuring of placements, etc.

Folkworks
Ros Rigby,
4 Black Swan Court,
Westgate Road,
Newcastle upon Tyne NE1 1SG.
☎ 091-222 1717.

Folkworks is the regional agency for the development of traditional arts, particularly in music and dance. Folkworks is involved with a range of educational activities and can provide advice and expertise in this area of arts practice. Folkworks works with Local Education Authorities and other agencies in devising education projects and workshops based on traditional music, song and dance.

Jazz Action
Adrian Tillbrook,
Jazz Development Officer,
Darlington Arts Centre,
Vane Terrace,
Darlington,
Co. Durham DL3 7AX.
☎ 0325-480 454.

Jazz Action may provide contact with professional jazz musicians who are available for instruction in improvising techniques, either to performing ensembles or to larger groups of either, or both, pupils and teachers.

Multicultural Arts Group
Ms Jane Hanlon,
Todds Nook School,
Monday Crescent,
Newcastle upon Tyne NE4 5BD.
☎ 091-273 3758 or 091-413 8212 after 5pm.

MAG encourages women from a variety of cultural backgrounds to become involved in the arts and crafts.

Newcastle Teachers' Adviser for Media Studies
Ben Moore,
Pendower Hall Teachers' Centre,
West Road,
Newcastle upon Tyne NE15 6PP.
☎ 091-274 3620.

Northern Association of Writers in Education
The Nanholme Centre,
Shaw Wood Road,
Todmorden,
Lancashire OL14 6DA.
☎ 0706-818419.

The prime movers in developing methods, procedures and a philosophy for Writers in Schools is the **Northern Association of Writers in Education (NAWE)**. Their membership consists of writers and educators. They publish the influential *Directory of Writers in Education*. To order a copy, contact the General Secretary.

Northumberland Schools Picture Loan Collection
Northumberland Arts Officer,
County Central Library,
The Willows,
Morpeth,
Northumberland NE61 1TA.
☎ 0670-512385.
FAX 0670-518012.

Part of the Schools Library Service, this facility enables schools to borrow work by local, regional and national artists for use by pupils and teachers. The collection is used in a variety of contexts including Northumberland Arts in Schools projects.

Sculpture North
Hebburn Centre,
Ellison Street,
Hebburn,
Tyne & Wear NE31 1YN.
☎ 091-428 0007.

Side Photography Gallery & Resource Centre
5/9 Side,
Newcastle upon Tyne NE1 3JE.
☎ 091-232 2208.

Youth and Music (North East)
Helen Dewhurst,
Washington Arts Centre,
Biddick Farm,
Washington,
Tyne & Wear NE38 8AB.
☎ 091-415 5334.
Youth and Music (North East) is an agency which promotes concert-going by young people with its Stage Pass concessions scheme, and is engaged in the provision of music in order to increase awareness and audiences amongst young people. They have experience in multi-cultural and regional entertainment. Events can be tailored to fulfil educational and social needs.

4. Local Arts Development Agencies

Establishing productive working relationships with local authorities is central to Northern Arts' strategy. A major means of pursuing this and of developing wider involvement in the arts has been the establishment of a network of Local Arts Development Agencies.

A LADA is defined as follows:

- it employs full-time professional arts staff.
- It promotes or develops the arts across a number of art forms.
- It is concerned with participation as well as presentation in the arts.
- It operates in a predefined geographical area.
- It attempts to fulfil a policy coherent with the aims, priorities and objectives of Northern Arts.

Educational work forms a part of the programme in many of these agencies.

LOCAL ARTS DEVELOPMENT AGENCIES & ARTS OFFICERS

Mary O'Malley,
Arts Development Officer,
Wear Valley District Council,
Leisure Department,
Springfield,
Willington,
Crook DL15 0HW.
☎ 0388-765555.

Andrew Rothwell,
Arts Development Officer,
City of Newcastle upon Tyne,
Central Library,
Princess Square,
Newcastle upon Tyne NE99 1DX.
☎ 091-261 0691.

Paul Gover,
Arts Development Officer,
Blyth Valley Arts Development Office,
93 Boudicar Terrace,
Blyth,
Northumberland NE24, 2JR.
☎ 0670-352036.

Ivan Sears,
Principal Arts Officer,
Department of Leisure & Tourism,
North Tyneside MBC,
Moor Park House,
Darras Drive,
North Shields NE29 8AT.
☎ 091-259 0944.

Andrew Ormston,
County Arts Development Officer,
Northumberland County Council,
County Central Library,
The Willows,
Morpeth,
Northumberland NE61 1TA.
☎ 0670-512385.

Sue Jenkins,
Arts Development Officer,
Borough of Barrow-in-Furness,
Piel View House,
Abbey Road,
Barrow-in-Furness,
Cumbria LA13 9BD.
☎ 0229-825500.

Andrew Bentley,
Arts Development Officer,
Middlesbrough Borough Council,
Recreation & Amenities Department,
P.O. Box 69,
Vancouver House,
Central Mews,
Gurney Street,
Middlesbrough,
Cleveland TS1 1EL.
☎ 0642-245432.

Sarah Maxfield,
County Arts Development Officer,
Cumbria County Council,
Education Department,
5 Portland Square,
Carlisle,
Cumbria CA1 5PU.
☎ 0228-23456.

Mo Dobbie,
Arts Worker,
Teesdale Enterprise Agency,
39 Galgate,
Barnard Castle,
Co. Durham DL12 8EJ.
☎ 0833-31851.

George Stephenson,
Chief Leisure & Publicity Officer,
MidNAG
(Mid Northumberland Arts Group),
Town Hall,
Ashington,
Northumberland NE63 8RX.
☎ 0670-814444.

Andrea Stark,
Head of Unit,
Sunderland Arts Development Unit,
Biddick Farm,
Fatfield,
Washington,
Tyne & Wear NE38 8AB.
☎ 091-417 6213.

Alistair Snow,
Director,
Cleveland Arts,
P.O. Box 12,
Marton House,
Borough Road,
Middlesbrough,
Cleveland TS4 2YP.
☎ 0642 211347.

Adam Sutherland,
Arts Development Officer,
Easington District Council,
Council Offices,
Easington,
Co. Durham SR8 3TN.
☎ 091-527 0501.

Amanda Ward-Baker,
Arts Development Officer,
Sedgefield District Council,
Green Lane,
Spennymoor,
Co. Durham DL16 6JQ.
☎ 0338-816166.

Bill Sinclair,
Arts Development Officer,
Langbaurgh Borough Council,
Kirkleatham 'Old Hall' Museum,
Kirkleatham,
Redcar,
Cleveland TS10 5NW.
☎ 0642-479500.

Stephen Hollier,
Arts Development Officer,
Hartlepool Borough Council,
Civic Centre,
Hartlepool,
Cleveland TS24 8AY.
☎ 0429-266522.

Cara McMahon,
Director,
Queen's Hall Arts Centre,
Beaumont Street,
Hexham,
Northumberland NE46 3LS.
☎ 0434-606788.

Peter Bevan,
Director,
Darlington Arts Centre,
Vane Terrace,
Darlington,
Co. Durham DL3 7AX.
☎ 0325-483271.

Steve Cowton,
Arts Development Officer,
Alnwick Playhouse,
Bondgate Without,
Alnwick,
Northumberland NE66 1PQ.
☎ 0665-510785.

Ken Cameron,
Rosehill Theatre,
Moresby,
Whitehaven,
Cumbria CA28 6SE.
☎ 0946-692422.

Paul Sherwin,
General Manager,
Carnegie Arts Centre,
Finkle Street,
Workington,
Cumbria CA14 2BD.
☎ 0900-602122.

Martin Weston,
Arts Development Officer,
Derwentside District Council,
Louisa Leisure Centre,
Front Street,
Stanley,
Co. Durham DH8 0TE.
☎ 0207-230311.

Hazel Hague,
Administrator,
**Durham Community Arts
Association,**
Fowlers Yard,
Back Silver Street,
Durham DH1 3RA.
☎ 091-386 8176.

Frank Wilson,
Director,
Dovecot Arts Centre,
Dovecot Street,
Stockton-on-Tees,
Cleveland TS18 1LL.
☎ 0642-611625.

Mike White,
Arts Development Officer,
Gateshead MBC,
Central Library,
Prince Consort Road,
Gateshead,
Tyne & Wear NE8 4LN.
☎ 091-477 3478.

Anne Pierson,
Director,
Brewery Arts Centre,
122a High-water,
Kendal,
Cumbria LA9 4HE.
☎ 0539-725133.

Ron McAllister,
Director,
Maltings Arts Centre,
Eastern Lane,
Berwick-upon-Tweed,
Northumberland TD15 1DT
☎ 0289-330661.

Nick Jones,
Eden Arts Trust,
The Watermill,
Little Salkeld,
Penrith,
Cumbria
☎ 0768-81523.

David Wilson,
Arts Development Officer,
South Tyneside MBC,
Central Library,
Prince George Square,
South Shields,
Tyne & Wear NE33 2PE.
☎ 091-427 1717.

Mick North,
Arts Development Officer,
Department of Leisure Services,
Carlisle City Council,
Civic Centre,
Carlisle,
Cumbria CA3 8QG.
☎ 0228-23411.

B.

1. National Arts Bodies

CRAFTS

The Crafts Council
Susie O'Reilly,
Education Officer for Schools and Young People,
44a Pentonville Road,
London N1 9BY.
☎ 071-278 7700.
FAX 071-837 6891.

The Crafts Council is the national agency for the development of the crafts, and in that sense all its work is educational. The Council produces *Craftslink* – a comprehensive guide to craft exhibitions, publications, visual resources, professional craftspeople, information and educational services available through the Crafts Council in England and Wales. Details available from the Education Section.

PHOTOGRAPHY, FILM & VIDEO

The British Film Institute
Maurial Alvarado,
Head of Education,
21 Stephen Street,
London W1P 1PL.
☎ 071-255 1444.

BFI Education's aim is to enable as many people as possible to discover new ways of thinking about, producing and enjoying the media, particularly film, video and television. Working with people in formal education, from primary to university level, in the community at large and in many other institutions.

THE ARTS COUNCILS

Arts Council of Great Britain
14 Great Peter Street,
London SW1P 3NQ.
☎ 071-333 0100.

The Arts Council of Great Britain has a small Education unit which can provide advice and information on current national developments in the field of arts and education. It is also able to assist in providing documentation on models of good practice and other information on arts in education. However, the responsibility for supporting artists in schools projects lies with individual RAAs and enquiries relating to this should not be directed to the Arts Council of Great Britain.

There are separate Arts Councils for Scotland, Wales and Northern Ireland:

Scottish Arts Council
12 Manor Place,
Edinburgh EH3 7DD,
Scotland.
☎ 031-226 6051.

Welsh Arts Council
Holst House,
Museum Place,
Cardiff CF1 3NX,
Wales.
☎ 0222-394711.

Arts Council of Northern Ireland
181a Stranmillis Road,
Belfast BT9 5DU,
Northern Ireland.
☎ 0232-663591.

2. National Research and Funding Agencies

ARTISTS IN SCHOOLS RESEARCH AND FUNDING BODIES

The Calouste Gulbenkian Foundation
98 Portland Place,
London W1N 4ET.
☎ 071-636 5313/7.

The Calouste Gulbenkian Foundation is an influential independent trust which:

- has carried out research into the provision of arts in schools – including the use of professional artists.

- published *The Arts in Schools: Principles, Practice and Provision*, in 1982 – which contains a very helpful section on artists in schools.

- provides funding for arts in schools initiatives.

National Foundation for Educational Research (NFER)
Dr Clare Burstall, Director,
The Mere,
Upton Park,
Slough,
Berkshire SL1 2DQ.
☎ 0753-74123.
FAX: 0753-691632

The NFER has recently completed a two-year study of the work of artists in schools. The researchers visited a wide range of projects in primary, secondary and special schools throughout England and Wales. As a result, a practical handbook has been produced, aiming to help teachers and artists to work together in the visual, verbal, performing and media arts. The book includes guidance for every stage of a project, from initiation, through planning, implementation and the development of the project after the artist's visit has ended. There is information and advice on funding, evaluation, multi-cultural projects, and working with children with special educational needs.

National Foundation for Arts Education (NFAE)
Professor Ken Robinson,
Director,
Department of Arts Education,
University of Warwick,
Westwood,
Kirby Corner Road,
Coventry CV4 7AL.
☎ 0203-524175.

The NFAE grew out of the **Schools Curriculum Development Committee**'s Arts in Schools Project. Its purpose is to offer practical support to schools in improving provision in the arts for all children and young people. Many of its projects had regional, as well as national impact – and made use of visiting professional artists. It published *The Arts in Schools Project* – a newsletter of up-to-date events and techniques. NFAE runs an information service for its members. Membership costs £15 (1990).

National Curriculum Council
Veronique Knighton,
Information Officer,
Albion Wharf,
25 Skeldergate,
York YO1 2XL.
☎ 0904-622533 ext. 283.
FAX 0904-622921.

3. Regional Arts Associations (RAAs)

There are currently twelve Regional Arts Associations in England
covering the whole of the country. At the time of going to press
major changes in the structure and funding of the Regional Arts
Associations were underway. When implemented in October 1991
these changes will result in the creation of ten new Regional Arts
Boards to replace the existing RAAs.

North West Arts is to be merged with Merseyside Arts to create
one RAB, Arts Board North West, while Lincolnshire and
Humberside Arts will be merged in two directions, with Lincolnshire joining Eastern Arts to become the new Eastern Arts Board
and Humberside joining Yorkshire Arts to become the Yorkshire
and Humberside Arts Board. Buckinghamshire joins Southern
Arts while West Sussex joins South East Arts. The following
description of RAA structures and roles will therefore be subject to
change but represents the position at the time of going to press.

Each RAA is an independent organisation funded by the Arts
Council of Great Britain, the British Film Institute, the Crafts
Council and local authorities within its region. While there is a
great deal of common practice, policies for arts in education differ
greatly between RAAs and between art forms.

RAAs may offer advice on planning, funding and other
information on artists in schools. Many RAAs are devising a
computer index of artists willing to take part in schools projects –
many already hold comprehensive lists of artists in schools. Most
RAAs also have a photographic index representing the work of
artists, photographers and craftspeople in their region. Several
publish newsletters or magazines – check your own RAA for the
latest information.

Some RAAs have Education Officers and may be able to deal
direct with enquiries from schools, others may not be able to
respond to individual requests for advice and assistance. To find
out more about an RAA's policies for arts in education you can
make contact by using the address list on the next three pages.

NOTE: **Changes in the structure will come into effect in
October 1991.**

East Midlands Arts
Forest Road,
Loughborough,
Leicestershire LE11 3HU.
☎ 0509-218 292.

Area covered: Derbyshire,
Leicestershire, Northamptonshire
and Nottinghamshire.

Eastern Arts
Cherry Hinton Hall,
Cherry Hinton Road,
Cambridge CB1 4DW.
☎ 0223-215355.

Area covered: Cambridgeshire, Essex,
Hertfordshire, Norfolk and Suffolk.

Greater London Arts
Coriander Building,
20 Gainsford Street,
London SE1 2NE.
☎ 071-403 9013.

Area covered: Greater London.

Lincolnshire & Humberside Arts
St Hugh's,
Newport,
Lincoln LN1 3DN.
☎ 0522-33555.

Area covered: Lincolnshire and
Humberside.

Merseyside Arts
Graphic House,
Duke Street,
Liverpool L1 4JR.
☎ 051-709 0671.

Area covered: Merseyside, District of
West Lancashire, Ellesmere Port and
Halton Districts of Cheshire.

North West Arts
12 Harter Street,
Manchester, M1 6HY.
☎ 061-228 3062.

Area covered: Greater Manchester,
High Peak District of Derbyshire,
Lancashire (except West), Cheshire
(except Ellesmere Port and Halton).

Northern Arts
9-10 Osborne Terrace,
Jesmond,
Newcastle upon Tyne NE2 1NZ.
☎ 091-281 6334.

Area covered: Cleveland, Cumbria,
Durham, Northumberland and Tyne
& Wear.

South East Arts
10 Mount Ephraim,
Tunbridge Wells,
Kent TN4 8AS.
☎ 0892-515210.

Area covered: Kent, Surrey and East
Susex.

South West Arts
Bradninch Place,
Gandy Street,
Exeter,
Devon EX4 3LS.
☎ 0392-218188.

Area covered: Avon, Cornwall, Devon,
Dorset (except Districts of
Bournemouth, Christchurch and
Poole), Gloucestershire and
Somerset.

Southern Arts
19 Southgate Street,
Winchester,
Hampshire SO23 9DQ.
☎ 0962-55099.

Area covered: Berkshire, Hampshire, Isle of Wight, Oxfordshire, West Sussex, Wiltshire, and Districts of Bournemouth, Christchurch and Poole.

West Midlands Arts
82 Granville Street,
Birmingham B1 2LH.
☎ 021-631 3121.

Area covered: Hereford and Worcester, West Midlands, Shropshire, Staffordshire and Warwickshire.

Yorkshire Arts
Glyde House,
Glydegate,
Bradford,
West Yorkshire BD5 0BQ.
☎ 0274-723051.

Area covered: North, South and West Yorkshire.

New Arts Boards to be created from October 1991:

Eastern Arts Board   *Address as Eastern Arts above.*

Arts Board North West   *Address as North West Arts above.*

Yorkshire & Humberside Arts Board   *Address as Yorkshire Arts above.*

There are also three Welsh Regional Arts Associations:

North Wales Arts Association
10 Wellfield House,
Bangor,
Gwynedd LL57 1ER,
Wales.
☎ 0248-353248.

Area covered: Clwyd, Gwynedd and District of Montgomery in the County of Powys

South-East Wales Arts
Victoria Street,
Cwmbran,
Gwent NP44 3YT,
Wales.
☎ 06333-875075.

Area covered: South Glamorgan, Mid Glamorgan, Gwent, Districts of Radnor and Brecknock in Powys and Cardiff

West Wales Association
Dark Gate,
Red Street,
Carmarthen,
Dyfed SA31 1QL,
Wales.
☎ 0267-234248.

Area covered: Dyfed and West Glamorgan.

4. Other National and Regional Arts Agencies

MULTICULTURAL ARTS GROUPS

Black Arts Alliance
Co-ordinator,
c/o 111 Burton Road,
Withington,
Manchester M20 8H2.
☎ 061-445 4168.

Assists with the promotion of Black art and artists (African, Caribbean, South and East Asian) in all art forms. Not a commissioned agency, simply there to put the establishment in touch with the artists, and when required help co-ordinate projects, performances and exhibitions. Experience with Social Services projects. Mainly concerned with multi-media projects.

Arts in Education for a Multicultural Society (AEMS)
Director,
Commonwealth Institute,
Kensington High Street,
London W8 6NQ.
☎ 071-603 4535.

Curriculum development project putting anti-racist/multicultural policies into practice through workshops and in-service training in schools and colleges, primarily led by practising professional black artists. Producers of resource lists and a Directory of Artists for Education. Initiators of a national arts education project.

Minority Arts Advisory Service
Beauchamp Lodge,
2 Warwick Crescent,
London W2.
☎ 071-383 4531.

CREATIVE WRITING
Multicultural Writers

Commonword Ltd (Cultureword Inc)
c/o 21 Newton Street,
Cheetwood House,
Manchester M1 12F.
☎ 061-236 2773.
This group has powerful community links in the North-West. They will help schools to promote black and women writers, and also to find funds and go about the procedure of placements.

Story-tellers

RAAs will usually hold the address of a local contact from The Guild of Story-tellers. Members of this group are highly active in schools country-wide.

Tell Tales
Lucy Wilson   ☎ 061-860 4659.
Parvinder Sohal   ☎ 0254-382964.
Heather Crawford ☎ 061-226 7962.
Tell Tales is a Manchester-based storytelling team for the age range 4-17 incorporating mime, dance, puppetry, music and audience participation. Phone for more information.

National Community Folktale Centre
Middlesex Polytechnic,
All Saints,
White Hart Lane,
London N17 8HR.
☎ 081-368 1299.
Register available only.

Verbal Arts

The Kitley Trust
Rosie Ford,
Director,
38 Bower Road,
Sheffield,
South Yorkshire S10 1ER.
☎ 0742-682115.
Founded 1990 to promote the art of writing in *all* fields by *whatever* means – workshops, conferences, readings, activism on the ground and in the institutions.

Verbal Arts Association
c/o 4 Clifton Court,
Cleveland Road
Huddersfield HD1 4PV.
West Yorkshire.
The Verbal Arts Association (VAA) promotes the role of writers in schools who can encourage oral skills in all subjects. They publish a wide-ranging information pack, full of techniques and ideas – the *VAA Information Pack: Teaching and Practising Verbal Arts in Education and the Community*.

Children's Writers

Children's Writers and Illustrators Group
Diana Shine,
Secretary,
84 Drayton Gardens,
London SW19 9SB.
☎ 071-373 6642.
This is a subsidiary organisation of the Society of Authors for writers and illustrators of children's books.

Writing and Science

Poetry Network International
David Morley,
Head Office, c/o 100 Cundy Street,
Walkley,
Sheffield S6 2WN,
South Yorkshire.
☎ 0742-340901.

Provides information and contact names of writers experienced in education. Committed to breaking down barriers between science and arts. Workshops provide new techniques for learning in subjects across the curriculum. The Network offers skill-sharing workshops for writing within the sciences, social sciences and technology.

Poets in Schools

Poetry Society Education Department
Education Officer,
21 Earls Court Square,
London SW5 9DE.
☎ 071-373 2551.
The Poetry Society works to promote poets and poetry and runs the Poets in Schools Scheme, sponsored by W.H. Smith; the education and examinations department brings poets to schools, teachers, children and students. The Education Department also maintains a directory of poets who are interested in schools work, in addition to running a number of poetry projects for young people.

Arvon Foundation (North)
Susan Burns & Marc Collett,
Centre Directors,
Lumb Bank,
Heptonstall,
Hebden Bridge,
West Yorkshire HX7 6DF.
☎ 0422-843714.

Arvon Foundation (South)
Julia Wheadon,
Senior Administrator,
Totleigh Barton,
Sheepwash,
Beaworthy,
Devon EX21 5NS.
☎ 040 923-338.
Arvon provides the opportunity for young people to live and work with established writers in an informal atmosphere, being treated as writers not pupils during the course.

Taliesin
Sally Baker Jones & Elis Gwyn Jones,
Administrators,
Tŷ Newydd,
Llanystumdwy,
Cricieth,
Gwynedd LL52 0LW.
☎ 0766-522811.
Taliesin is Wales' recently opened writing centre modelled on the Arvon Foundation.

Schools Poetry Association
David Orme,
27 Pennington Close,
Colden Common,
Winchester,
Hampshire SO21 1UR.
☎ 0962-712062.

Bloodaxe Books
Andrew McAllister,
Publicity Manager,
P.O. Box 1SN,
Newcastle upon Tyne NE99 1SN.
☎ 091-232 5988.
FAX 091-222 0020.
Britain's premier poetry publishing house is based in the North East, and has published over 200 poets, many of whom are freelance writers who work in schools and can be contacted through Bloodaxe. Bloodaxe also promotes the annual Evening Chronicle Poetry Competition in the Northern region and publishes many relevant poetry books. A new schools poetry anthology edited by Helen Dunmore is forthcoming.

DANCE
National Resource Centre for Dance
Research Officer,
University of Surrey,
Guildford,
Surrey GU2 5XH.
☎ 0483-509316.
FAX 0483-300803.
Provider of resource materials to assist with the study and practice of dance. Facilities include an information service, dance archive, courses and publications.

National Organisation for Dance and Mime
Jane Attenbrough,
9 Rossdale Road,
London SW15 1AD.
☎ 081-788 6905.
NOFDAM represents the professional dancers.

Community Dance and Mime Foundation
Lucy Pearman,
Administrative Director,
Leicester Polytechnic,
Scraptoft Campus,
Scraptoft,
Leicester LE7 9SU.
☎ 0533-418517/551551.
FAX 0533-419659.
National service organisation and development agency for those working in the field of community dance and mime. Offers training courses and initiatives plus information and advice.

ADiTi: YYY
National Organisation of South Asian Dance
The Administrator,
6th Floor,
Metrochange,
Hall Ings,
Bradford,
West Yorkshire BD1 5SG.
☎ 0274 754090.
ADiTi was set up to provide a focus and help develop an infrastructure for South Asian dance. It works as a development/information agency and can offer advice on South Asian dance and music. In its capacity as an information agency ADiTi can provide details of South Asian dancers and musicians and the work options they offer. Their work can cover performance, workshops, residencies, work with special needs in both educational and community settings.

**Council for Dance Education
and Training**
James Ranger,
Director,
5 Tavistock Place,
London WC1H 9SS.
☎ 071-388 5770.

**National Association for Teachers
in Further and Higher Education
(Dance Section)**
Gordon Curl,
Chair,
Copse End,
Conyngham Lane,
Canterbury,
Kent CT4 5JX.

**National Dance Teachers'
Association**
Veronica Jobbins,
Chair,
Islington Sixth Form Centre,
Benwell Road,
London N7 7BW.

**Standing Conference on
Dance in Higher Education**
Valerie Briginshaw,
Chair,
West Sussex Institute
of Higher Education,
Bishop Otter College,
College Lane,
Chichester,
West Sussex PO19 4PE.

Academy of Indian Dance
Tina Cockett,
Education Worker,
16 Flaxman Terrace,
London WC1 9AT.
☎ 071-387 0980.
The Academy of Indian Dance is a
charitable trust which aims to promote the practice and appreciation of
Indian Dance, particularly in an educational context. It offers a variety of
educational programmes for schools
and colleges including workshops
and residencies, lecture demonstrations, and in-service training for

teachers. Workshops for primary
schools are topic based and linked to
the National Curriculum. For secondary schools projects are aimed at
enhancing and developing the movement content of Performing Arts and
Dance Courses.

Black Dance Development Trust
Clarence Chambers,
4th Floor,
Rooms 34-35,
39 Corporation Street,
Birmingham B4 4LG.
☎ 021-631 3808.

**English Folk Dance and
Song Society**
Cecil Sharp House,
2 Regents Park Road,
London NW1 7AY.
☎ 071-485 2206.

Mime Action Group
Penny Maze,
Battersea Arts Centre,
Old Town Hall,
Lavender Hill,
London SW11 5TF.
☎ 071-441 0349.

DRAMA

**Standing Conference of Young
People's Theatre**
Belgrade Theatre,
Coventry CV1 1GS.
☎ 0203-256431 ext. 240.

Independent Theatre Council
Assistant Administrator,
Unit 129,
West Westminster Business Square,
Durham Street,
London SE11 5JA.
☎ 071-820 1712.
The Independent Theatre Council is
the Managers' Association, represen-
tative and advisory body for Indepen-
dent Theatre companies throughout
Great Britain and exists to
strengthen, protect and develop the

field of work. Schools may advertise for company services in its monthly newsletter which is circulated to all its members.

National Council of Theatre for Young People
Durham Buildings,
Regent College,
Inner Circle,
Regents Park,
London W1.

National Association of Youth Theatres
Centre Co-ordinator,
Midlands Arts Centre,
Cannon Hill Park,
Birmingham B12 9QH.
☎ 021-440 2930.
An umbrella organisation, not itself a youth theatre, but open for all youth theatres to join. The Association produces a monthly newsletter, organises conferences and workshops, has a resource and script library and offers general help and advice.

National Association for the Teaching of Drama
Jane Holden,
Chair,
Backworth Drama Centre,
Church Road,
Backworth,
Newcastle upon Tyne NE27 0JE.

MUSIC

UK Council for Music Education and Training
Linda Cummins,
13 Back Lane,
South Luffenham,
Oakham,
Leics LE15 8NQ.
☎ 0780-721115.
FAX: 0780-721401.

PHOTOGRAPHY, FILM & VIDEO

The organisations listed in this section will all give advice, professional contacts and ideas for projects:

Council for Education Technology
3 Devonshire Street,
London W1N 2BA.
☎ 071-580 7553.

Educational Television Association
The King's Manor,
Exhibition Square,
York YO1 2EP.
☎ 0924-433929.

The National Museum of Film, Photography & Television
Princes View,
Bradford,
West Yorkshire BD5 0TR.
☎ 0274-727488.

OTHER ORGANISATIONS

Association for Business Sponsorship of the Arts
2 Chester Street,
London SW1X 7BB.
☎ 071-235 9781.
ABSA administers BSIS – the Business Sponsorship Incentive Scheme – which may match funding obtained from private sources for artists in schools projects. ABSA can also advise on private companies with a special interest in supporting arts in schools work.

National Educational Resource Information Centre
David Taylor,
Maryland College,
Leighton Street,
Woburn,
Bedfordshire MK17 9JD.
☎ 0525-290364.

**Centre for Arts Research and
Development**
Malcolm Ross & Hilary Radnor,
Directors,
c/o School of Education,
University of Exeter,
St Lukes,
Exeter EX1 2LU.
☎ 0392-264829.
FAX 0932-263108.
Research into Arts Education in
schools and the broader community.
Special focus on aesthetic develop-
ment, curriculum content, assess-
ment and evaluation. Will undertake
consultations, lectures, demonstra-
tions and commissions.

**National Association for
Education in the Arts (NAEA)**
Linda Cummins,
Secretary,
13 Back Lane,
South Luffenham,
Oakham,
Leis LE15 8NQ.
☎ 0780-721115.
FAX: 0780-721401.

Group for Education in Museums
The Secretary,
63 Navarino Road,
London E8 1AG.
☎ 071-249 4296.

**National Society for Education
in Art and Design (NSEAD)**
David Jones,
Assistant General Secretary,
7a High Street,
Corsham,
Wiltshire SN13 0AS.
☎ 0249-714825.
FAX: 0249-716138.

5. Publications and Reports

REPORTS

The following are available from the Arts Council of Great Britain (address on page 69):

Dance and Mime Artists in Education
Sandra Hockey (June 1987).

Dance Artists in Education
Report of a Pilot Project 1980.

Dance Pack
Information on resources major companies offer and guidelines.

Writers in Schools
Sue Harries. A report on the scheme in England up to 1983.

The Arts and the Education Reform Act 1988: *What teachers and artists need to know*
Published by the Centre for the Study of Comprehensive Schools: CSCS, University of York, Heslington, York YO1 5DD. ☎ 0904-433240

The Art Works Report
A report following a course for people with art training to enable them to acquire skills in workshop techniques to use with community and special needs groups. Available for £3.50 from: Shape London, 1 Thorpe Close, London W10 5XL. ☎ 081-960 9245.

The Future of the Arts in Schools
Edited by Andrew Worsdale. A report of the NCC Arts in Schools project's national conference. Available for £1.50 from the National Foundation for Arts in Education.

The Value of the Artist
A report on the conference staged by North West Arts, attended by art advisors, artists, heads and teachers in Greater Manchester. The conference's primary aim was to promote the value of artists' work in schools and colleges. Available from North West Arts, 12 Harter Street, Manchester M1 6HY.

PUBLICATIONS

The following publications are available from the National

Foundation for Arts Education, Department of Arts Education, University of Warwick, Westwood, Kirby Corner Road, Coventry CV4 7AL:

Architects-in-Schools
By Nigel Frost (RIBA, 1987). Published by the Royal Institute of British Architects, 66 Portland Place, London W1N 4AD. ☎ 071-580 5533.

Artists and Schools
This publication has brought together information gathered during the Arts in Schools schemes. It deals with placements involving verbal and visual art and textiles and offers advice on planning residencies based on past experience.

NFAE, University of Warwick, Westwood, Kirby Corner Road, Coventry CV4 7AL. ☎ 0203-524175. Code Aas. £5 (subscribers £4).

AEMS Directory of Artists for Education
A new directory of artists from African, Caribbean, Asian, South Asian, Chinese and Latin American traditions working in education. Available for £10 from: AEMS, Commonwealth Institute, Kensington High Street, London W8 6NQ.

Artists in Schools: *a handbook for teachers and artists*
By Caroline Sharp and Karen Dust. A practical comprehensive guide for teachers and artists working or intending to work together in schools in any art-form, and with any age group. Available for £8.95 from: Plymbridge Distributors Ltd, Estover Road, Plymouth PL6 7PZ. ☎ 0752-705251.

The Arts 5-16
Three publications by the Arts in Schools project published by the National Curriculum Council (1990) which offer practical guidance to delivering the arts in schools. *A Curriculum Framework* covers the main issues for curriculum planning and assessment in the arts and offers ideas for the development of school arts policies. *Practice and Innovation* has approaches to a range of practical issues; based on the experience of schools taking part in the Arts in Schools project. *A Workpack for teachers* has ideas and resources for organising in-service workshops with primary and secondary staff and for use in initial training courses. All three available from Longmans Resources Unit, ☎ 0904-425444.

The Arts in Education: *some research studies*
Edited by L. Tickle, published by Croom Helm (1987).

The Arts and Schools
HMSO, for the Office of Arts and Libraries and the Department of Education and Science. A compilation of short, illustrated case studies of artists of various disciplines working with schools.

The Arts in Schools
By Ken Robinson. A study into the Arts in Education, out of which came the Arts in Schools project. Available for £6 from: The Calouste Gulbenkian Foundation, 98 Portland Place, London. W1N 4ET. ☎ 071-636 5313.

Arts in Schools Project
Bulletin No. 9, December 1988. Schools Curriculum Development Committee, c/o NFAE.

British Music Education Yearbook 1990/91
Edited by Annabel Carter. Includes details of new publications, performers in education, in-service courses, youth concession schemes and a section on music technology. Available for £9.95 (plus £1 p&p) from Rhinegold Publishing, 241 Shaftesbury Avenue, London WC2H 8EH. ☎ 071-240 5740.

The Creative Tree
Edited by Gina Levete (1987). A practical guide to setting up arts projects, geared particularly towards people who may be disadvantaged in some way, but also applicable to educational work. Examples from all over the world and an international directory of ideas and contacts. Available for £6.95 from Michael Russell (Publishing) Ltd, The Chantry, Wilton, Salisbury, Wiltshire.

Dance in the School Curriculum
A leaflet on the place of dance within the school curriculum, for headteachers and curriculum planners, jointly prepared by the Council for Dance Education and Training, National Association of Teachers in Further and Higher Education, National Dance Teachers' Association and Standing Conference on Dance in Higher Education. Available from (send 22p SAE): Council for Dance Education and Training, 5 Tavistock Place, London WC1H 9SS.

Dance Pack
A useful resource with update available from the Dance Department of the Arts Council: £6.50 for the pack, £3.50 for the update.

Directory of Northern Writers
Provides information for those wishing to contact writers based in Cleveland, Durham, Tyne & Wear, Cumbria and Northumberland. From: MidNAG, Town Hall, Ashington, Northumberland NE63 8RX.

Education for Art
By Rod Taylor, published by Longman.

The Future of the Arts in Schools
Report of the final conference of the project £1.50 (free to subscribers).

Jazz Education
By M. Greig. Published by Jazz Services and the Arts Council (1989), this gives details of regional jazz-in-education projects and contacts.

The Magic Exercise
By Victoria Neumark. This publication offers valuable advice and experience based on twelve case studies of residencies run in arts centres. Available for £8.95 from: ADA, The Arts Centre, Vane Terrace, Darlington DL3 7AX. ☎ 0325-465930.

Making School-Based Inset Work
By P. Easen, published by Croom Helm (1985).

Making Ways: *the visual artist's guide to surviving and thriving*
By David Butler. This publication is aimed at artists, with a useful chapter on residencies and how to become involved with or organise one. The advice in this chapter is useful to both those seeking residencies and those offering them. Available for £11.95 from: AN Publications, P.O. Box 23, Sunderland SR4 6DG. ☎ 091-567 3589.

Northern Association of Writers in Education Directory
The most comprehensive guide to writers experienced in the field, this publication is updated biennially and contains guidance on how to set up and evaluate writers' residencies. Available for £3.00 from: The General Secretary, NAWE, The Nanholme Centre, Shaw Wood Road, Todmorden, Lancashire UL14 6DA. ☎ 0706-818419.

NAWE News
The newsletter of the Northern Association of Writers in

Education. Published three times a year, it contains documented examples of residencies, ideas for good practice, updates on funding opportunities, and all the latest techniques. Sample copies available from: NAWE, address as above.

Residencies in Education
By Daniel Dahl & edited by Susan Jones. A similar publication to *Under the Rainbow* produced by Yorkshire Arts for schools and artists in the Yorkshire region. Available from: AN Publications, P.O. Box 23, Sunderland SR4 6DG. ☎ 091-567 3589.

Resources for Arts Education for a Multi-Cultural Society
A practical guide to resources available to teachers, advisers, community groups and artists for use in multi-cultural arts education projects. Available for £2.50 from AEMS, Commonwealth Institute, Kensington High Street, London W8 6NQ.

SOURCE BOOKS FOR GRANTS AND SPONSORS

Funding can be gained from the most unlikely sources. With careful research – and imagination – you might be able to find money from any number of grant-making trusts for your project. Three essential reference books give you the detailed information on trusts, grant-making policy and a comprehensive listing of grant-making bodies and the fields of activity they are likely to support. Copies may be available in a local library:

A Guide to the Major Grant-Making Trusts (1986)
Available from: Directory of Social Change, Radius Works, Back Lane, London NW3 1HL.

Directory of Grant-Making Trusts (1987) (10th edition)
Available from: Charities Aid Foundation, 48 Pembury Road, Tunbridge Wells, Kent TN9 2JD.

The Educational Grants Directory (1988)
Edited by Luke Fitzherbert & Michael Eastwood.
This is a guide to voluntary and charitable help for children and students in need. Available for £12.50 from: Directory of Social Change, Radius Works, Back Lane, London NW3 1HL.

Abbreviations

ABSA	Association for Business Sponsorship of the Arts
ACGB	Arts Council of Great Britain
BAA	Black Arts Alliance
BSIS	Business Sponsorship Incentive Scheme
CC	Crafts Council
CDT	Craft, Design and Technology
EC	European Community (formerly EEC)
ESG	Educational Support Grants
GCSE	General Certificate of Secondary Education
GRIST	Grant-related In-service Training
INSET	In-service Training
LEA	Local Education Authority
LEATGs	Local Education Authority Training Grants
LMS	Local Management of Schools
NAWE	Northern Association of Writers in Education
NCC	National Curriculum Council
NFER	National Foundation for Educational Research
PTA	Parent Teacher Association
RAA	Regional Arts Association
RAB	Regional Arts Board (from 1991)
SCDC	School Curriculum Development Committee
SDO	Staff Development Officer
TRIST	TVEI-related In-service Training
TVEI	Technical and Vocational Education Initiative
TVEEX	Technical and Vocational Education Extension
VAA	Verbal Arts Association

APPENDICES

10 Stages in Setting Up and Running an Artist-in-School Project

AN ORGANISER'S CHECKLIST

1. *Decide on*
☐ AIM OF PROJECT.
☐ LENGTH AND STYLE OF PLACEMENT.
☐ WHICH ARTIST: Information from experience of other teachers, RAA, LEA, directories, listings etc.
☐ ESTIMATE COST: Range of current fees from RAA.

2. *Contact artist*
☐ OUTLINE AND DISCUSS REASONS FOR AND STYLE OF PLACEMENT.
☐ OFFER RANGE OF DATES (one, two or three terms in advance).
☐ DESCRIBE TARGET GROUP: number, age and ability/ previous experience of pupils.
☐ ESTABLISH FEE AND LIKELY EXPENSES.

3. *Calculate Detailed Budget*
☐ ARTIST'S FEE (including preliminary visits).
☐ EXPENSES.
☐ MATERIALS.

4. *Make Approaches for funding to (using strong well-argued case).*
☐ SCHOOL: Subject or department capitation, inter-departmental capitation, school or Head's fund, PTA fund, Governor's fund, School INSET funding.
☐ LEA: Specific arts funding if available, LEATGs, ESG funding, TVEI or TVEEX funding.
☐ LOCAL & NATIONAL SPONSORSHIP: Local or district council money for libraries, arts and leisure activities (if a shared event with community), industry, trust funds, government schemes, EEC grants.
☐ RAA: Funding may be available under umbrella of education/ specific art form/issue-led funding.

(Funding may be secured by a partnership arrangement of two or more of these agencies.)

5. Confirm placement with artist and funding agents.

6. Hold Preliminary meetings, with

☐ ARTIST (if possible): visit school, meet staff and pupils; plan details of project including accommodation, payment (if long term scheme, is an interim payment required?), is tax to be deducted at source or by the artist?, materials required.

☐ HEADTEACHER & OTHER STAFF: to inform about purpose, examine issues of supervision, check timetables change, discuss press release.

☐ PUPILS: to prepare for project.

☐ PARENTS: to inform and seek any necessary release.

(Either a series of single meetings or a joint meeting.)

7. Finalise details of resources, space, time, staff role, etc.

8. Secure funding, draw up and sign agreements/contracts as necessary.

9. Run project and monitor throughout.

☐ ISSUE PRESS RELEASE (and invite media coverage if required).

☐ DOCUMENT PROJECT AS IT HAPPENS.

☐ PERIODIC REVIEW (if long term placement).

☐ INVITE VISITORS (if appropriate): other pupils, staff, parents, funding body representatives, school governors, LEA Inspectors, other schools.

10. Conclusion: Evaluate and hold summary event.

☐ INFORM *ALL* THOSE INVOLVED OF THE OUTCOME: send reports or invite to concluding event.

☐ PAY ARTIST (promptly).

☐ FOLLOW UP WORK: negotiate with artist, and implement.

APPENDIX 2

14 Points to Consider in Drawing Up a Contract

☐ The artist's legal position relating to responsibility for children's safety, etc.

☐ Insurance cover, for example for the artist's work or belongings (equipment) when in school.

☐ Public liability insurance.

☐ Rates of pay.

☐ Approximate times and dates of work.

☐ Provision of raw materials.

☐ Indication of space.

☐ Responsibility for administration.

☐ Education/legal restrictions on employment.

☐ Conditions of service in schools.

☐ Requirements of project.

☐ Responsibility of school.

☐ Required documentation.

☐ Copyright and reproduction issues.

AUTHORS PUBLISHED BY

BLODAXE BOOKS

*For a complete list of poetry, fiction, drama and photography books
published by Bloodaxe, please write to:*

**Bloodaxe Books Ltd, P.O. Box 1SN,
Newcastle upon Tyne NE99 1SN.**

David Morley was born in Lancashire in 1964 and is a professional biologist. He has published two books of poems, *Releasing Stone* (1989) and *A Belfast Kiss* (1990). He is currently finishing a book of translations of Mandelstam for Littlewood Press while working on a third collection.

In 1989 he received a major Eric Gregory Award from the Society of Authors, a Tyrone Guthrie Award from Northern Arts, and won the Northern Poetry Competition and The Poetry Business Pamphlet competition. His work is included in *Poetry Introduction 7* (Faber, 1990), *Northern Poetry One* (Littlewood Press, 1989), *The Gregory Poems 1987-1990* (Hutchinson, 1990) and *The New Lake Poets* (Bloodaxe Books, 1991).

He has held residencies in many schools throughout England and was Vice-Chair of the Northern Association of Writers in Education. He lives in Sheffield.